Punditry & Prose

Frank's Frank'nsense

Punditry & Prose

Frank's Frank'nsense

Cover art by Josefine Tilton

Revised edition July 2019.

ISBN-13: 978-1985132610

ISBN-10: 1985132613

Library of Congress Cataloging in Publication Data

Tilton, Frank W, 1943 –

Punditry & Prose

Published by Create Space, Amazon Properties

Other Books by Frank Tilton

Eternity

Grappling with God and Grammar

How to Cope with those Middle School Years

The Qanaq Conundrum

What? No Babies?

Kindermanns Komet (German Language)

Preface

If Frank Tilton's writings are anything, they are eclectic. Much like his life experiences. Much like his education. Much like the books he reads, the music he chooses, the ideas in his cranium.

In this book are pieces I have written. Most are editorials (almost every one of them published in the Winchester Star, Winchester, Virginia).

Some are responses to questions my grandchildren have asked. Or should have asked.

Some are ruminations. We septuagenarians do tend to ruminate, after all. Whatever they are, I choose to leave them behind for my progeny and perhaps yours. Hence this book

Editorials, as opinion pieces, reflect my own views. You are welcome to disagree. Still, keep this in mind. There is *opinion* and there is *informed opinion.* The distinction matters. For more on this, read **On Opinion** (see Contents).

Curriculum Vitae

This is the page where you the reader find what the author wants you to know about himself. Typically, you'll see Ph.D., Dissertation, a list of books and articles published, and a list of memberships in professional organizations. Some of which they've actually attended within the past fifteen years. All this so you'll know you really ought to read what they have to say. I don't mean to belittle anyone here. If they walk the walk of what they talk and talk, fine. They might be worth attending to. Some are.

But, I, too, have Curriculum Vitae. And here they are (notice the plural):

* grocery clerk (long before items were "scanned")
* chicken farm ranch hand (or was that chicken ranch farm hand?)
* filling-station attendant (when window washing and a check of the oil was standard service)
* gold mine dynamiter's assistant
* gold ore crusher operator
* backwoods firewood splitter
* rattlesnake exterminator (self-defense only)
* telephone solicitor (lasted only one-day, detested it)
* UPS route driver
* typist for an Italian attorney (when keyboards were mechanical not electrical, and there was no spell-check)
* Air Force Morse radio operator

* sports writer, sports editor, news writer, newspaper editor
* Air Force historian (real books, some classified)
* public affairs officer, USAF (24-year USAF career)
* college instructor, English and Journalism
* assistant professor teaching international officers
* teacher, 9th grade English and middle school German, 19 years
* husband, father, grandfather .... whoa!
* resident of California, Colorado, Montana, upstate New York, downstate Texas, Nebraska, Indiana, Virginia and a few other places such as Italy, Germany (both sides of the Iron Curtain), Libya (before Kaddafi), Egypt, Greenland, and oh my, the memory fades.
* All right! I'll fess up. Yes, I've also garnered one Bachelor's degree in English, another in German, a Master of Science in radio-television, and state teaching certification for English, German, and Journalism, all at the secondary level.
* And, no. I do not have a Ph.D. I needed some time in there for rattlesnake exterminating, firewood splitting, and those pesky little wads for the dynamiting.

Contents

On Opinion

Opinions are like shoes. Some shoes are stylish and colorful but aren't the sort of footwear you'd want to walk a mile in. Others are of quality leather and crafted for support and comfort, and, yes, for walking far more than a mile. I could set this up as a quality vs. style dichotomy, but truth be told, both have their place and time. Stylish wins with formal attire; support and comfort win for day-to-day and distance.

So it is with opinion. Some gets by just fine in stand-alone mode, like stylish shoes. Some needs quality support to gain credibility.

In my Preface I made the statement: There is *opinion* and there is *informed opinion.* I wasn't just being loftily academic. There is a difference. And the distinction is important.

Consider this:

> George says: Best car on the planet, that Chevy Camaro.
> Phillip asks: Really? Have you ever driven one?
> George says: Not yet. But that's a really hot car!

Now consider this:

> Al says: Best car on the planet, that Chevy Camaro.
> Fritz asks: Really? Have you ever driven one?
> Al says: This is my third one. Been driving these for 20 years. I've had over a 100,000 miles behind the wheel of each one. Terrific car!

Okay. No contest, right? Al has given us an *informed opinion.* George not so much.
So, if you apply this model to your listening and reading skills, you'll have little trouble recognizing which opinion you find more credible. True with Camaros. True with politics. But not so true with soda pop.

Soda pop brings us to another variety of opinion – *personal preference.* Like the stylish shoes, personal preference has its time and its place. Your friend likes Coca Cola. You'd rather drink Pepsi. You can imagine the conversation, right? You and your friend could debate all day, but chances are at the grocer you'd both buy the product you prefer. It's a matter of taste. Personal preference. But not always! It's possible your beverage choice is based upon *informed opinion.* For example, if your concern is caffeine, you might choose either Coca Cola (39 mg) or Pepsi (38mg) over Mountain Dew (54mg). If sugar content is important to you, you'd likely select, Coca Cola (44g) or Pepsi (41g) over Mountain Dew (46g). A little more research might lead you to shop for a diet soda. The point remains*: informed opinion is one thing, and personal preference is another.*

With examples like Camaros and Colas it may seem of little importance to you, this matter of *opinion* whether informed or otherwise. Not so! In today's world of misinformation, disinformation, media manipulation and downright skullduggery much is at stake. That's why it is critical to recognize opinion in all of its forms. For a prime example of *informed opinion,* go to the article *About those Democrats.*

Elsewhere in this book, I have addressed the opinion topic, but this would be a good place for a bit of minimum review:

> Any statement positing what is good, better, or best, (or any synonym of these) is opinion. Likewise, the word *will*. *Will* is future tense, and neither you nor I know factually what *will* happen tomorrow much less ten-minutes from now. Should, must, and ought are words of advice, hence opinion. Many adjectives - especially those ending with –able, -ible or -less - are opinion words.

Finally, let's go back in history, to a time when folks could disagree with civility. A decade or so before or after the American Civil War, there was a British essayist by the name of John Stuart Mill. This fellow wrote a piece called *On Liberty*. He offered some advice I wish we'd heed these days. He wrote:

- Opinions ought never to be suppressed.
- There are three sorts of beliefs (opinions) that can be had—wholly false, partly true, and wholly true—all of which benefit the common good.
- If any opinion is compelled to silence, that opinion may, for aught we can certainly know, be true.
- Though the silenced opinion be an error, it may, and very commonly does, contain a portion of truth.
- Since the general or prevailing opinion on any subject is rarely or never the whole truth, it is only by the collision of adverse opinions that the remainder of the truth has any chance of being supplied.

- Even if an opinion be true, it must be vigorously and earnestly contested (in the interest of it being accepted and understood) so as not to be lost, or enfeebled, and deprived of its vital effect. (I have ever so slightly edited this last point to modernize it a bit without losing the intent.)

Today's college and university campuses would surely benefit (*yes, this is an opinion - mine*) by returning to Mill's recognition of the value of hearing-out opinions, even, or especially, those with which one might disagree. Such civil listening, however, is not much in evidence at this time.

About those Democrats

Want to attempt something difficult? Try talking with your grandkids about facts and politics. Problem is, facts are not the most popular of ingredients in today's dialogs (true for grandkids, true for adults). Yet I remain convinced that given facts my grandchildren are capable of a rational understanding of issues. It probably helps that the youngest of them is beyond high school age.

Before we examine facts, let's agree to keep in mind such things as campaign promises, stated priorities, and party platforms.

Facts: Looking back from 2016 to 1931, the Democratic Party held the majority of both the House and the Senate for 62 years. During those same 85 years, the Republican Party held the majority in both houses for 22 years. So, from the Hoover presidency to the Obama presidency Democrats controlled Congress more than two-thirds of that time span.

Given a Democrat-controlled Congress for 62 of the past 85 years and given Democratic Party Presidents for 48 of those years, it ought to be easy to see the results of their leadership. Actually, it is easy. All we need to do is compare promises with results.

Let's begin with education. Facts: In 2015, fully 73 percent of Detroit's 8th grade students failed to achieve basic proficiency in math skills. Those same Detroit students performed at only 44 percent proficiency in reading. And Philadelphia, Baltimore, and Cleveland ought not boast about scores at 58, 51, and 48 indicating scarcely half of their students can read at proficient levels.

So, what have these academic scores to do with Democratic Party majority for more than six decades? It should be readily apparent. Failure. Failure of promises. Deficiency of leadership. And this despite another fact: Per CNBC.com "Two-thirds of America's 100 largest cities are controlled by Democratic Party mayors."

Let's shift our focus to economics. Fact: Detroit was declared bankrupt on December 3, 2013, with its $18.5 billion debt. Fact: Illinois, according to valuewalk.com, "has $15 billion in unpaid bills, and has entered its fifth straight year without a budget. This has created a devastating situation for social programs within the state.... The prospect of an Illinois bankruptcy appears inevitable." Fact: The Democratic party since 2004 holds the majority in both houses of the Illinois General Assembly. No budget?

One final gut-wrencher. Crime. Fact: In 2016, Chicago suffered 751 killings by gunshot. This year to date 318 have similarly fallen and 1,821 have been shot in Chicago although the year is but half complete. Now recall the April 2015 Baltimore riots and the high crime rates of Cleveland, Detroit, and Philadelphia.

Education, economics, crime. Dismal failure. And how does this relate to those 62 years of Democratic majorities? Consider these 2016 Presidential election results favoring Democrat candidates: Chicago (83%), Detroit (68%), Baltimore (84%), Philadelphia (82%), and Cleveland (75%).

These voters are victims of embezzlement. Votes delivered. Promises unfulfilled.

Fact: There is an inverse correlation between Democrat promises and Democrat results.

On the Second Amendment

> *A well regulated Militia, being necessary to the security of a free State, the right of the people to keep and bear Arms, shall not be infringed.*
> -- Second Amendment

The chief reason we today fail to understand the Second Amendment as written by our nation's founders is that we have a dire shortage of school-marms.

Years ago, when school-marms taught grammar, students could not progress to the next grade unless they understood the rudimentary functions of English grammar. This is clearly no longer a required skill. If it were, there would be much less confusion about the meaning of our Second Amendment.

The 27 words of that amendment made good sense to those who crafted our Constitution. Made sense for two reasons. They had been taught grammar. They had also learned the lessons of history. One must either guarantee rights, or one will forfeit them. These authors of our Constitution had just defeated King George III, and they knew quite well the necessity of a *militia* to guarantee freedom.

It is that correlation between *Militia* and the *security of a free state* that explains the reason for the Second Amendment. That's why this amendment's first thirteen words explain *why* our citizens need the *right to bear arms.* Consider now the grammar.

Our sixth-grade school-marms taught us that *being* is a present participle and that a participle is a verb doing the work of an adjective. Hence, *being necessary to the security of a free State* is a participial phrase. This kind of phrase modifies a noun.

So, what noun is being modified (think: clarified, specified, limited)? Well, that is clearly the word *Militia.* We see, then, that the right to keep and bear arms does not exist in a vacuum. It is connected to an obligation, that of guaranteeing *the security of a free state.*

And this is why we today must not hesitate to consider limitations, even certain reasonable restrictions, when it comes to now urgent questions of guns and rights. The 39 signees of our Constitution clearly recognized this as they crafted those first thirteen words. Just under half of this amendment it is devoted to limiting the purpose of freely bearing arms.

Were they fools, these founders of our nation? I think not. But I'm not sure I can say the same for those today who should, but do not, apply the same lessons of grammar as did Washington, Madison, Franklin and three-dozen others.

Our courts and such organizations as the NRA have long chosen to ignore those first 13 words and focus exclusively on the remaining 14. Those emphasizing freedoms.

Though I am an NRA member, I also understand the grammar and the intent of our forefathers.

Those gentlemen did not propose to unleash 19-year-olds armed with automated weapons-of-war into our school classrooms. But they did write our Second Amendment by beginning with limitations.

That is why our state, local, and federal legislators must not fear to establish fair and reasonable limitations and restrictions as we now begin to debate anew. We all know what must be done. Let us not hesitate.

Parting thoughts: It might be time to bring back school-marms. It might likewise help if politicians knew that sportsmen do not use combat assault rifles for deer hunting.

-30–

On Washington

Washington Must Be Recycled!

Who among us is not convinced? *Houston, we have problems. In Washington.* You, I, and our neighbors could without a doubt quickly jot a list of ten such "problems." Chances are good that my list, your list, and those of our respective neighbors would share six if not seven items. Oh, the order might differ. But the likelihood is great that the words *taxes, budget, Congress*, *political*, and maybe even *Constitution* and *election* would appear on your list as well as mine.

Fact is most of us are fed up with what we see happening in Washington. I know I am! And near the top of my list would be the word *obfuscation*! Okay, so maybe that particular word didn't show up on your list. But I'd bet some part of this word's definition is on your list: *to make something obscure or unclear, especially by making it unnecessarily complicated.* Sure, some things by their very nature are complicated. But not all things must be so. Do members of Congress intentionally overcomplicate issues so as to obscure their true intent? Well, your response is as good as mine. But let's return to that list of problems.

If you feel frustrated by what Congress does, or fails to do, have you ever heard yourself ask, "What can we do about it?" Stop fretting! There are things we can do! And they are not complicated ... if enough of us agree to do what needs to be done. The "what to do?" is truly not complicated, nor is it difficult. Vote twice! Once in the primaries! Then in the general election. And in both "votes," simply do this: Elect no Incumbents. Presto! That's called Term Limits!

You can do it.
I can do it.
We must do it.

And it does not require amending the Constitution!

-30-

What Congress Must Do Now

Let's face it. More needs fixed than a simple budget reduction-debt ceiling bill. I've listed below "Ten immediate steps" but even these, and the pending budget-debt bill will mean nothing as long as members of Congress continue to "ear mark" the "I want to be re-elected" tweaks. If this nation is serious about a long-term budget fix, we will elect only those who pledge "no ear marks." Further, and I don't wish to play the "NIMBY" game here, but millions of us seniors were "taxed" to pay into Social Security, were "taxed" upon receiving Social Security, and will not sit by idly while "ear marks" and other short-sighted budget decisions continue to deplete the budget while Social Security is trimmed to "address" the grim budget shortfall.

Ten immediate steps:

1. 25% across-the-board budget reductions for all Executive Branch department staffing, and 25% reduction all Congressional salaries.
2. 90% reduction in travel budgets, all Executive Branch departments.
3. Eliminate permanently all forms of "ear mark" (pork barrel) legislation.
4. 100% reduction (complete cessation) of Congressional retirement plan. Replace existing plan with Congressional participation in Social Security.
5. Separate "disability" and all other "non-retirement elements" from Social Security (in effect returning to pre-Johnson era plan for Social Security.)

6. 100% reduction (complete cessation) of Farm subsidies followed by re-instituting the program – if needed – for only those agri-businesses with a documented 10-year record of agri-business sales.
7. Maintain payments at current level to Social Security, Medicare, and military current retirees; plan reductions for future retirees on a gradual scale.
8. Enact immediately a 25% Federal sales tax (fair tax) across-the-board, no exceptions, no deductions.
9. Enact immediately a 5% Federal income tax across-the-board, includes corporations, no exceptions, no deductions. Concurrently, scrap all existing income and capital gains taxation.
10. Reduce IRS staffing by 90% (following steps 8 and 9 above).

These ten immediate steps are not a "wish list." They are the demands of the American people, who, you ought not to forget, are your employers! Prepare to pack your bags and depart Washington if you ignore these demands. Term limits begin now! We will elect no incumbents!

An Open Letter to Stephen Hawking (published on publisher's web page):

Sir, with all due respect to you and to your scholarly and scientific achievements, I am compelled to ask you to re-examine the logic, if not the science, from which you have derived this statement: "Because there is a law such as gravity, the universe can and will create itself from nothing."

At best, we can state that gravity is a force. Though we can neither see nor physically examine gravity, we can to a limited extent measure it. Yet, we can "measure" gravity only with respect to matter. Without some form of matter, gravity would remain indiscernible. Matter, then, is the sine qua non of gravity.

It follows that both matter and gravity exist. It also follows that the two are mutually dependent. Science, Professor Hawking, has established that we humans can neither create nor destroy matter (law of conservation of mass or matter). Science has also told us that we humans cannot create or destroy energy - though we are able to change energy from one form to another (first law of thermodynamics).

Logic also tells us that self cannot create self. Gravity did not create gravity. Matter did not create matter. That brings us to "source." If gravity is, as you say, a law, then it has an author, that is to say, a source. And since matter did not create matter, it, too, has a "source." And, Professor Hawking, that which has a source is not "spontaneous." So, we find ourselves, Sir, seeking that which man from his earliest days has sought. The source.

You, Congress, are Fired!

Congress got the "message" last election, but failed to "heed" that message. So, Congress, in the words of a certain well-known business exec, "You're fired!"

Beginning today, the "voters" of this country will do what you, Congress, have failed to do: We, the voters, will solve the problem! Here is how. We will:

- Vote in the primaries! and, Elect no incumbents!
- Vote in November 2012! and, Elect no incumbents!

Guess what! This is called "term limits." Term limits in four easy steps! We, the voters, already have the power to limit your terms. And we promise to do so. And this, Congress, is your "pink slip." This is your notice of termination of your employment! You see, we, the voters, do not need to amend the Constitution. Nor do we need "demonstrations." We simply will vote you out of office. That's why we will:

- Vote in the primaries! and, Elect no incumbents!
- Vote in November 2012! and, Elect no incumbents!

You, Congress, have failed. Again.
 You are FIRED!
You have forgotten who you work for.
 You are FIRED!
You have failed to trim the size federal government.
 You are FIRED!
You have failed to balance the budget.
 You are FIRED!

You have failed to pass federal funding legislation within established deadlines.

You are FIRED!

You have failed to tax all Americans equally.

You are FIRED!

You have failed to disengage Congress from "special interest" groups.

You are FIRED!

You have placed "party" priorities over "national" priorities.

You are FIRED!

You have continued "ear-mark" or "pork barrel" legislation for your constituents.

You are FIRED!

You have continued to campaign for your own re-election when you should be addressing the needs of this country.

You are FIRED! You are FIRED! You are FIRED!

We, the voters, will

- Vote in the primaries!
- Elect no incumbents!
- Vote in November 2012!
- Elect no incumbents!

We can and will replace 100% of the House and all Senators who are running for re-election. Pack your bags, Congress. We not only want change, we will change! Starting with Congress!

-30-

Dear Senator Warner

re: S.1323, a bill to express the sense of the Senate on shared sacrifice in resolving the budget deficit.

I am compelled by events, in particular the pending budgetary measures facing you, the 112th Congress, to emphasize certain very basic points. Hence this missive.

But first, I urge you --- via your staff who will first view this entreaty - not to quickly discard this into the "pile" of messages from "disgruntled constituents." I may be a disgruntled constituent, but I am one who fully recognizes that it is within my power to remove you and your fellow legislators from office. I am cognizant of the fact that I am your employer, that I provide your salary and benefits, and that I can and will terminate your employment should that become necessary. And I am seething with discontent over the demonstrated inability of the 112th Congress to adequately address the needs of this Nation!

That said as a preface, I shall simply make the following clearly stated points:

* I oppose plans to reduce Social Security and Medicare benefits to current retirees. (This is not a routine "NIMBY" response. You need to recognize that I - and others like me - have paid "taxes" - whether or not we opted to do so -- into these programs. In my case, I paid into both of these programs for more than 45 years, and I paid at the higher end of the then existing scales.)

* I oppose the lack of distinction between "retiree" benefits and "welfare" support.

* I vehemently oppose the use of Social Security funding for "disability" programs.

(What I oppose is not that funds are made available to the disabled, but rather the source of those funds.)

* I oppose Federal funding (my tax contributions) in support of the following items:

-- Planned Parenthood

-- Public Broadcasting

-- Farm subsidies *see note

-- Embryonic stem cell research (stem cell, yes. embryonic, no.)

* I propose:

1. Trim 10% across-the-board from the federal budget.
2. Trim 90% from federal travel budgets
3. Reduce (both staffing and budget) by 80% these Executive Branch Departments:

--Department of Agriculture

--Department of Commerce

--Department of Education

--Department of Energy

--Dept. of Health, Human Services

--Department of Housing and Urban Development

--Department of Labor

--Department of the Interior

--Department of the Treasury

4. If legislation for a new program requires funding, reduce existing programs to fund it.

5. Adopt a flat 5% income tax for all individuals, all business, no deductions.

6. Adopt a flat 5% federal retail sales tax. All items. No exceptions.

7. Honor commitments to military veterans, senior citizens.

8. Get the federal government out of the health-care business, the education business, and business (oversight, yes, operating, no).

9. Let state governments run the states. If you mandate state action, pay for it.

10. Use tax credits to help rebuild this nation's transportation and energy infrastructure.

*Note regarding farm subsidies: Discontinue the program in its entirety. Then, reestablish the program only for those farm businesses which have a documented business record of having produced food crops for a period to include the five years prior to the receipt of subsidies. In brief: farm subsidies are to be payable only to those who actually produce farm products as their chief means of livelihood.

These steps, Sir, outlined above, are the basis upon which I will evaluate your performance. Should your performance fail to achieve these goals, I, and many others of like mind, will terminate your current employment.

Thank you, and Respectfully yours

What's a Democrat, a Republican, a Conservative, a Liberal?

Looking back at my youth, I did not know (and still don't) which political party my father favored, if either. Some of his assertions (rare) left me thinking he was Republican. Others were more in tune with Democrats. The first election I took interest in was that of John Kennedy vs. Richard Nixon. I wasn't old enough to vote, but the year after Kennedy's 1960 election, I entered the Air Force. Being young, I identified with Kennedy and had a certain distaste for Nixon even though I came from Nixon's hometown of Whittier. The Nixon family was not universally well-liked within his hometown. I was in the Air Force only two months when the Berlin Wall went up and solidified the existing Iron Curtain border. My first post-training assignment was in Italy with what then was called Security Service. I quickly became aware of world events and my own role in them. I had attained the ripe old age of 18, and voting age was then 21. The Berlin crisis, the 1962 Cuban Missile Crisis, the Vietnam War followed one after the other and took me quickly from interested observer to active participant in national and international affairs. The first election I voted in was 1968 -- Nixon vs. Humphrey. By this time I was a seasoned 25-year-old and had learned to distinguish between Democratic and Republican characteristics. Moreover, I well knew the importance of foreign policy, and so I voted for Nixon, probably in part because I knew he had served eight years as vice-president under Eisenhower, whom I held in high esteem. Humphrey had been Vice President under Lyndon Johnson. As time and elections went by, I became increasingly aware of the differing values of "liberals" vs.

"conservatives" though it took me longer to grasp the idea that a conservative Democrat was not so far removed from a liberal Republican. Because I was born and raised in the West (California), I failed to perceive that "Southern" Democrats (conservative) were, for all practical purposes, Republicans. They would not "be" Republicans, however, because that was the party of Lincoln and Grant (Civil War, north). Still, though I at first favored Johnson's efforts in the realm of civil rights (and I remain supportive of that, though I make the distinction between opportunity and achievement), I began to perceive the true costs of his "Great Society" programs. That was what, over time, led me to better perceive the characteristics of "liberal" vs. "conservative." Now jumping forward many years, that very question, liberal vs. conservative, remains the "dividing line" regarding politics. I try to sort it out by setting up a dichotomy similar to this (remember to think "tends to" rather than in "absolutes") However, a list like this serves a limited purpose since many people, myself included, identify in part with portions of both lists, and both major political parties have conservative and liberal adherents. In truth, our nation is an amalgamation of both, and both have merit:

(See table next page)

Conservative	**Liberal**
Government is enabler	Government is caretaker
Man is self-sufficient	Man is dependent on government
Health care is business	Health care is government role
Oppose long-term welfare	Support welfare
Policies favor free-enterprise	Policies favor consumer
Environmental policy favors business	Environmental policy favors creatures
Foreign policy favors strategic interests	Foreign policy responds to"issues"
Sees U.N. as failed institution	U.S. obliged to support U.N.
Opposes abortion	Favors abortion as woman's right
Favors tax decrease to stimulate economy	Favors government spending to stimulate
Lower tax, smaller government	Higher tax, larger government
Suspicious of government power	Sees government as benevolent
Liberty over equality	Equality over liberty
Focus on individual	Focus on community
School vouchers: parent choice	Increase public school funding
Death penalty as punishment	Abolish death penalty, rehabilitate criminals
Favors gun ownership	Favor gun control
Acknowledge God, Creator	Oppose religious expression in government
Oppose same-gender marriage	Favor legalized same-gender marriage

Congress/Government: Problems

Ethics & Standards of Conduct:

The concepts here are relatively simple, but they are frequently ignored. Even when not ignored, the lines differentiating between what is "right" or "wrong" or "legal" or "illegal" will often be blurred.

Simple concept:

If you are employed by someone, you are obligated to use both **time** and **resources** to the benefit of the employer.

Time: The <u>time</u> for which you are "employed" belongs to the employer.

Resources: The property, building, equipment, supplies, money, utilities (electricity, water, heating, cooling) and sometimes vehicles (cars, trucks, aircraft) belong to the employer.

When <u>you use</u> the employer's **time** or **resources** for <u>personal use</u>, you are stealing.

Facts:

<u>All members</u> of the Federal government, whether elected or appointed, are employees (President, Congress, Senate, judges, and military and civilian staff members of all Federal agencies or departments).

They are employed by the "People of the United States."

They receive salary and benefits from the "People of the United States."

They are obligated to use both **time** and **resources** to the benefit of the employer, the "People of the United States."

If they use **time** and **resources** for personal gain or personal endeavors, they are violating the law.

There are literally hundreds of laws, directives, and published policies that specify detailed examples of legal or illegal activities.

(Note: These same obligations/laws apply to all levels of government whether individual states, counties, cities, townships, or school districts.)

Examples of Misconduct:

- A U.S. President is charged with personal misconduct while in his office. He uses his staff (legal advisors, secretaries, administrative assistants) to prepare documents, statements, press releases, and press conferences on his behalf.
- A U.S. Senator flies aboard a military aircraft to Europe to attend a conference. He tasks his staff to get tickets for himself and his wife to attend a Formula One auto race in Italy the weekend after the conference.
- A Federal judge uses his staff to do research, uses his office computer word processing software, and uses his office hours, all to write a novel he plans to publish.
- An Air Force commander uses a fighter jet and flies to Nellis Air Force Base near Las Vegas, Nevada, so that he can attend his daughter's wedding.
- A U.S. Senator pushes legislation for a fighter jet the military has not requested and does not want. The aircraft in question is produced in the Senator's state.

- A lobbyist pays (or gives gift, i.e. vacation travel) a Congressman in return for the Congressman's vote or sponsoring a bill favoring the lobbyist's business!

Other Examples of Misconduct:

- As State Governor: (from: CBS Chicago.com)

- Blagojevich was trying to get (himself) appointed Secretary of Health and Human Services in exchange for appointing Valerie Jarrett to President Obama's Senate seat.

- Blagojevich was trying to get Obama's help setting up a non-profit funded with millions of dollars, which Blagojevich could run after leaving office.

- Blagojevich was trying to shake down racetrack owner John Johnston for $100,000 in campaign cash in exchange for Blagojevich quickly signing legislation to benefit the racetracks.

- Blagojevich was trying to get $1.5 million in campaign cash from supporters of Jesse Jackson Jr. in exchange for appointing Jackson to the Senate.

- Blagojevich was trying to shake down Children's Memorial Hospital CEO Patrick Magoon for a $25,000 campaign fundraiser in exchange for approving a state funding for doctors at the hospital.

- Another State Governor uses a police helicopter to have himself flown to his child's soccer game.

- A bus-boy in a restaurant conceals himself for five-minutes (not official break time) and uses his own cell phone to call a friend.
- An I.T.T. employee uses a company-provided rental car while on business in Colorado; he drives the car to Des Moines, Iowa, to visit his cousin Zeke.
- An office worker uses the office computer and printer to print a term paper for a college course.

Need to Know: Alison Stewart

For Alison Stewart: I am most impressed (favorably) with your reporting having seen you recently (Need to Know). Unlike many in the media today, you ask questions in what (to my ear) is a balanced and neutral manner. That's the good news. However, in your report on a deep geologic nuclear waste-disposal site in New Mexico, you failed to ask a most relevant question. At the point at which you reported on cost of "above ground" waste containment, you should have asked for the identity of contractors building that containment equipment. That, together with relevant Congressional districts of the contractors, might have added greater understanding of who supports the above ground storage methods, and why. Always, always, follow the money trail! Thank you.

-30-

Pay heed, Washington

Let's make this simple so that Congress and the President will "get it."

1. Taxes: Tax all Americans at the retail level! No need to "tax the rich" or to "spare the poor."
One tax fits all. No loop-holes. No deductions.
2. Balanced budget: Expenditure in any year = revenue from the previous year.
3. Debt reduction: Pay 1% of annual Federal revenue toward the principal of national debt.
4. To fund debt reduction, reduce all Executive Branch department budgets by 2% each year for a period of 20 years. Reduce by 90% the staffing of IRS since with a retail tax IRS becomes superfluous.
5. Eliminate 100% "Farm subsidy" payments.

That's it. Five steps to attain Federal financial stability.
These are not suggestions. This is not a wish list!
This is a demand. Pay heed, Washington.
How do we voters bring this about?
Simple:

1. ELECT NO INCUMBENTS !
2. Elect only new candidates who commit, in writing, to these five steps.

A reader wrote

"No more taxpayer money flowing into the "Free Market System."

I wrote: I'm more concerned about taxpayer money flowing into the bottomless pockets of the Federal Bureaucracy. What flows into the "Free Market System" eventually flows back out in the form of products and jobs.

I surely agree with the remainder of what you are saying. We must take back Washington, and the only way we can do that is to vote "out" those who are now "in." It matters not a whit which party. And we must do that twice. Once in the primaries, and next in the generals. We must also do this in both 2012 and 2014. Only then will Congress get the message!

Message? We want fair tax (see fair tax dot org), we want a balanced budget, we want an end to "ear-marks," and we want folks in Washington who LISTEN to the people of this country (and as I used to tell my teenagers, the difference between "hearing" and "listening" is ACTION.)

These changes I speak of are not a dream. They can be reality, but only if you and I and about 200 million of the rest of us make it so.

Here is what we must do:

Join the "Million Voter March"
April 21-22, 2012
Shoe leather Democracy

We will: Re-cycle Washington!
We will: Elect No Incumbents!
We will: Change Washington!
We will: Cleanse Congress!

And after the march, we vote the deadwood out of Congress.

None of this requires changes to the Constitution. And none of this requires violence.

-30-

Proclamation to the 112th Congress

Made to both parties, both houses.

1. Get it right or we'll send you home.
2. Recognize that term limits are what elections are for; they do not require Constitutional amendment.
3. Avoid grandstanding. We demand hard work, not "hearings."
4. Do not spend time, energy, staff, or federal funds running for your own re-election.
5. Recognize that your re-election is not why voters (tax payers) sent you to Washington.
6. Stop "earmarks." Now!
7. Recognize that taxpayers from 49 states do not wish to fund a bridge in West Virginia.
8. Recognize that item 7 (above) is a metaphor. No offense to West Virginia
9. Use one-bill one-vote method. Vote for a "bill" not for a "rider."
10. Balance the budget. Now.
11. Trim 10% across-the-board from the federal budget.
12. Trim 90% from federal travel budgets (beyond the 10% in item 11 above.)
13. If legislation for a new program requires funding, reduce existing programs to fund it.
14. Adopt a flat 5% income tax for all individuals, all business, no deductions.
15. Adopt a flat 5% federal retail sales tax. All items. No exceptions.
16. Honor commitments to military veterans, senior citizens.

17. Get the federal government out of the health-care business, the education business, and business (oversight, yes, operating, no).
18. Let state governments run the states. If you mandate state action, pay for it.
19. Use tax credits to rebuild this nation's transportation and energy infrastructure.
20. Get to work! Now!

-30-

Ruminations of a Newcomer

It's happened to each of us. We find ourselves in a new town. A new state. We expect to experience what folks call "a learning curve." So we aren't really surprised at finding some things "new" and "different" from our former habitat But ...?

Things in Virginia just don't seem to be what they seem to be. The road map which assisted us in navigating our way to our new home clearly showed the "State" of Virginia. But no sooner did we exit Maryland than we found ourselves in the "Commonwealth" of Virginia! So much for roadmaps.

But we should have taken that as an oracle of things to come. For in the few weeks since we've become official residents of the "Common-state-wealth" of Virginia we've discovered the truth. Virginia's officialdom artfully dodges the issue altogether, or at least straddles the Civil War split-rail fence on the topic.

Evidence? Our newly acquired motor vehicle operator licenses are "Virginia Driver's Licenses." Ditto for our State "Department of Game & Inland Fisheries" fishing licenses. But - are you ready for this? - we have been issued a "Commonwealth of Virginia" Voter Card. So, now it's clear. We can go driving and fishing in the State of Virginia, but we must vote in the Commonwealth of Virginia.

Hmmmm. We worry about such things, we newcomers. I mean, what if we become incarcerated for a felony? Would we be imprisoned in a State prison or a Commonwealth prison? It might make a difference. I mean, who would want to eat State prison food when you might have the opportunity for Commonwealth prison food? If there is honor among thieves, surely there must be culinary compensation for being incarcerated in a Commonwealth clink.

But let's move on to something far more practical. Asking for directions. Nowhere are "Things in Virginia just don't seem to be what they seem to be" more apparent than in the matter of navigating the local streets and roads.

What we have yet to understand is how locals can keep a straight face about it all. They neither grin nor grimace when saying, "Sure. Just take Hummingbird lane here until you reach Red Rooster. Now, Hummingbird won't be Hummingbird by the time you get to Red Rooster because after crossing Grouchy Grouse, Hummingbird becomes White Whippoorwill."

He continued, "At Red Rooster be sure you turn right, not left."

"And why is that?" we inquired.

"Well, if you turn left Red Rooster becomes Burnt Bunting. It's been that way since Millard Fillmore was President. You have to turn right if you want Red Rooster."

"Well, do we want Red Rooster?"

"No, of course not, you want to go straight when you reach Red Rooster."

"Okay. We got it. We're at the intersection of White Whippoorwill and Red Rooster and Burnt Bunting. And we go straight on White Whippoorwill."

"Straight, yes. But not on White Whippoorwill."

"Not on White Whippoorwill?"

"No, because that's where White Whippoorwill becomes Burnt Bunting."

"I thought Burnt Bunting was the street not to turn left into at the intersection of White Whippoorwill and Red Rooster and Burnt Bunting."

"Yep, that's correct. But at this point, Burnt Bunting turns left and White Whippoorwill becomes Burnt Bunting."

At this point we smiled and thanked the gentleman. And as soon as he was out of sight, we switched on our car's navigator.

Meanwhile, we think we've got it all figured out. The "Common-state-wealth" of Virginia must have re-designated all these street names at the time Millard Fillmore was President.

Our logic? Well, Fillmore was a Yankee. The "Common-state-wealth" of Virginia had an inkling during Fillmore's Presidency that Yankees would someday soon be wanting to navigate their way to Richmond. And what better way to assure that asking for directions to Richmond would result in those Yankees reaching - instead - Baltimore!

So, now we understand. But, by the way, we're still looking for Sapsucker Lane. It was on the architect's plat we examined before we purchased lot 125 on Turnstone Lane. But to this day, we haven't found Sapsucker. Still, given our current experiences in this, our new "Common-state-wealth," we're sure to someday find Sapsucker Lane. It's probably on the opposite shore of Lake Frederick and connects to Hudson Hollow Road.

Be that as it may, we have, after but a few weeks residence in Frederick County, discovered the truth about Virginia's Commonwealth. It's sort of an "I live in a more upscale county than you do" kind of thing.

Turns out Loudon County - located on the eastern side of these Blue Ridge hills - has more "common" wealth than any other county in the state. Why, personal income over in Loudon County starts with seven-digit numbers. And that's just for the part-time newspaper delivery folks. I'm told that voters in a town just east of Leesburg have passed a referendum adding a "C" to the town's name. Soon the road maps will show the town of "Cashburn" where formerly "Ashburn" was adequate to their needs.

Bottom line is this: it's a "what's in a name" issue. Virginia's founders, having severed the apron strings binding them to the King of England, decided to establish a political community founded for the common good. But the title, the "Commongood of Virginia" didn't measure up to the

Loudon County self-image, so "Commonwealth" was adopted instead. At least, that's what we newcomers have deduced.

-30-

A Grandfather to a Grandson

A grandfather's ears are like radar. They detect movement and direction. At times those elderly ears discern that something might be "off course." Such was the case in recent days when one grandfather heard one grandson put forth a proposition that, "A candidate for office ought to be evaluated on the basis of technical expertise rather than upon ethical considerations of character."

Now, it could be that the grandson was uttering what he had heard in an academic setting, and that the proposition was solely rhetorical. Something to be put forth in a debate. Yet, it also might be that the grandfather's "radar" had detected movement along an azimuth leading to potentially catastrophic consequences.

Given that the 18-year-old grandson is soon to be venturing into the voting booth, the questions surrounding "candidates" and their "ethical qualifications" are no longer an academic exercise.

<u>Hence these grandfatherly thoughts on the matter:</u>

Nothing, make that NOTHING, is more important than a candidate's ethics, honesty, and truthfulness! Notice, please, that this statement does not include the word "religion." Humans are quite capable of behaving ethically, honestly, and truthfully with or without the influences of organized religions. All humans (even Shakespeare well knew this) have the capacity for good and for evil. Psychologists and other students of human behavior delight in delving into the "nature vs. nurture" questions posed by this dilemma. But, let us leave that topic to the social scientists for now, and take aim on the more practical considerations as they apply to candidates for public office.

Note first this from an English essayist: "There can be no friendship without confidence, and no confidence without integrity." - Samuel Johnson

Now before I offer examples clarifying why NOTHING is more important than a candidate's ethics, honesty, and truthfulness, allow me to make clear some differences between public office and private enterprise. You should not discern from these remarks that ethics, honesty, and truthfulness do not apply to those engaged in private enterprise, the world of business. Some of the examples I offer below will help make that clear. But there is a major difference to note: those engaged in private enterprise are using their own funds (or the funds of investors) while those engaged in public office are using public funding (my taxes and yours). Keep this in mind as we proceed. It is a distinction of major importance.

Let's begin with a hypothetical case

Students in a high school homeroom class decide to collect funds so that the class can offer a scholarship to the daughter of a firefighter who has perished while fighting a fire. All students contribute from their own resources: their own savings, portions of their earnings from part-time jobs, and funds they collect from other persons. The students elect classmates to take care of fund-raising responsibilities.

One of these is the project team leader, another is the treasurer, and another heads up publicity campaigns. Within six months they collect $15,000.00. They plan an event at which they will make the donation to a special bank account set up for the grieving family. One day before the event, however, they discover that their collected funds have disappeared. The treasurer explains that he invested the funds in the stock market, but that he lost rather than gained in the transactions. The funds are no more. Later, investigation reveals that the treasurer actually spent the $15,000.00 on a ski trip in the Canadian Rockies. He used public funding for his own self-interest. And, yes, the treasurer here is guilty of a crime: misappropriation of funds, theft, and fraud (the deception regarding having invested the money).

<u>Let's move to real-life cases</u>

The examples I'm offering here are reconstructions of actual events that did happen, do happen, and are presently happening. Anyone who so wishes can find published media reports which reveal such examples.

First recall, however, that whether elected or appointed, public officials are paid by the public to perform tasks for and on behalf of the public. In short, they work for the public. They are provided funding, resources, equipment, buildings, and employees (who themselves are public employees) with the specific intent that they use these things to benefit all citizens. They are "entrusted" with money and assets, our money and our assets. When they abuse that trust, misuse those assets, they are in violation of that trust, and often are engaging in criminal activity. That is why ethics, honesty, and truthfulness are of utmost importance as we consider candidates for public office.

Examples: (The term "office-holder" could be a President, a legislator (house or senate), a state governor, a mayor, or any other elected or appointed public official.) All of these are examples of wrong-doing, fraudulent activity, crimes, currently being done (or recently done) by "public officials."

- A candidate spends campaign funds to hide the fact that he has been having an affair with a woman.
- A candidate's assistant spends campaign funds to have his personal ''dream home" built.
- A governor collects "hidden payment" in return for his approval of a construction project. (Legally, he should approve or disapprove as a function of his office.)
- A congressman accepts a "campaign contribution" in return for his vote which provides federal funding for a construction contract. The donor (of the "campaign contribution") is the construction contractor!
- A senator spends taxpayer funding to pay expenses for his own re-election campaign.
- A White House cabinet member (federal employee) spends lavishly (public money) for personal "pleasures" while in Las Vegas (ostensibly on business.).
- A dozen White House security staffers (Secret Service) (yes, those are public employees using public money) spend money and time with prostitutes while they should have been arranging security for a presidential visit to Colombia.

- A senator votes for funding for "agricultural subsidies" when he, himself, is the recipient for such funds.
- A federal employee plans a trip to Alaska. He adds the "airline miles" to his own mileage account. Later he uses the "miles" for a personal trip for himself and his family. Incidentally, the trip to Alaska was not necessary. The "business" could have been conducted via teleconference.
- A senator pushes a bill through Congress to build a federal highway in his state when the highway itself is not needed. Huge amounts in federal funding are spent in his state, benefitting the senator (at reelection time). Those same funds could have been used to pay down the national debt.
- A President uses his staff (clerks, assistants, typists) and materials (time, paper, printing ink, computers) in an effort to defend himself in court for a personal wrongdoing.
- A federal employee attends evening college classes to gain a master's degree in business administration. During the day, while at work, he uses his office computer to do research for a term paper; he prints his research paper on the office computer.

There are other such cases. Most of these are examples of "embezzlement." If you do not know what embezzlement is, you, and all too many American taxpayers, are part of the problem. If you know that elected or appointed officials are doing these things, and you take no action, technically you are "aiding and abetting" a criminal in the commission of a crime.

These are ethical and moral issues. And, yes, voters should, and must, take such things as these into account when considering candidates.

If a man steals a little, chances are good he'll steal a lot.
If a man lies to his wife, chances are he will lie to the public.
If a man does not keep his commitments with his family, chances are he will not honor his oath of office.
If a man uses deception to get elected, chances are he'll use deception to remain elected.
If a man cheats to get through college, chances are he'll cheat when employed.

Hence, much more than technical expertise and "knowledge" is demanded of candidates for public office.

Keep this in mind when it is time to cast your vote.

-30-

Intelligent Reporters?

Why do "intelligent" reporters continually miss (or ignore) the basic facts of a story? The President "hits the road" to bolster his party's chances in a forthcoming election. At the same time, his Cabinet members travel to improvised "events" for the same purpose. An "intelligent" reporter would note: that Federal employees who are paid with Federal tax dollars are using their time, their resources, their staffs, and their office equipment, pursuing not the goals of the Executive Department to which they are assigned, but rather, are blatantly campaigning in support of one party's candidates! Want evidence? Check the calendars of the Secretaries of Commerce, Interior, Labor, and every other Cabinet-level department. An "intelligent" reporter would do that. And an "intelligent" attorney would know what to do with that information.

Or, is "intelligent reporter" an oxymoron?

Or maybe an oxymoron without the "oxy"

-30-

Misinformed!

You, Sir, could scarcely be more misinformed! (re Mark Stern, *Private Sector Needs Government*, Monday, June 25, 2012). I can only hope that your students are of such stock that they can differentiate between what you say and what truly is the case.

You state: *It is the government-created infrastructure that the private sector uses to underpin the jobs that it creates.*

Reality: Government-created infrastructure is possible only with government-collected revenue. The source of government-collected revenue is twofold; the first is private sector businesses, and the second is employees of private sector businesses and those of government itself. Government levies taxes upon both businesses and employees. That is the source of revenue for government-created infrastructure.

You state: *Government subsidies underpinned the development of the railroads and the airlines....*

Reality: Without revenue from private sector business and its employees, there could be neither government subsidies nor government employees to administer those subsidies.

You state: *Government has created the basis for wealth across much of America.*

Reality: Investors willing to risk private funds create the basis for wealth. Government does not create wealth; government collects and redistributes wealth.

The closest you come to a valid statement is when you write: *(Government) must be a partner with free enterprise.*

Reality: Only when government and private enterprise work in a cooperative manner is there the possibility of synergistic growth that benefits both. When business is healthy, government can be healthy. Government policy that spurs business growth is the means of creating government revenue.

-30-

To Marcinko, the Rogue Warrior

I just finished reading Rogue Warrior, and because I'd be at the bottom of Demo Dick Marcinko's list of credible sources (being Air Force, you know), I'd appreciate it if you'd forward my brief comments to him.

First, I could not agree with him more with respect to his views on committing American men to combat. There can be no goal other than defeating the enemy! Completely! No negotiation. Terms of peace are dictated when combat is finished. But that, of course, has not happened since 1945. If our leadership is not committed to total defeat of the enemy, whatever the level of combat, then don't waste the lives of our men!

Second, I was at, and part of, Wadi Kena (big fat airplanes with mushrooms mounted on the top) prepping for Eagle Claw. Okay, so I have all the combat skills of a junior Boy Scout who flunked out of Webelos, but I did what I was trained to do. And like Marcinko, that day of failure remains etched in my memory. The combination of shame, grief, and anger makes for lousy bedfellows. I was back at Ramstein on the date of the mission and could not look my fellow NATO guys in the eye. Worst day of my 24-year career! And yet, out of that dark cloud came SEAL Team 6. For that I am grateful.

Like Marcinko, I started enlisted, finished commissioned and have no tolerance for fools! Unlike Marcinko, I have no combat experience. That does not, however, limit my admiration or my gratitude for those who have paid that price. Thanks for that, for the internal warfare with bureaucrats, and for the book! Greetings to Gold Dust Frank.

Kicking Nonsense in the Kiester

She has it right, as in correct. So does he. But before we identify the specific she and he, let's address some very basic issues.

Let's start with this question: when, oh when, will we stop this nonsense? We stand by idly, or we sit upon our ever-widening buttocks, while allowing nonsense to run rampant. Which nonsense, you ask? Try this one from the Saturday, September 5, 2015, Winchester Star. We are told on page A3, that "a federal judge has denied a transgender teenager's request" to use the school bathroom of his choice. Or her choice.

I applaud that judge, identified as Robert G. Doumar of the Eastern District of Virginia, though my reasoning and his may differ in the particulars. I applaud him for kicking nonsense in the kiester! (Kiester, also spelled keister, is slang for buttocks, and if kiester was good enough for President Ronald Reagan, it remains good enough for me.) The particular nonsense receiving Judge Doumar's boot in his September 4 ruling is the fact that we Americans have apparently lost our ability to distinguish between science and feelings.

A teenage student, born female, now feels that she ought to be considered a boy. She prefers to use the boys' bathroom at school. Now, I'm going way "out on a limb" here. I realize that some voices will rise up to call me homophobic. I'll be lambasted for hate crime! Well, I'll just have to take that risk. Much like Kim Davis of Rowan County, Kentucky. She is currently "in jail" paying the consequences for her civil disobedience. I applaud her. And now you know the identity of both the "she" and the "he" of my opening statement. I am not homophobic. But I am ready to kick nonsense in the kiester!

Why? Because we have students and parents who value their feelings greater than they value the rights of others. I am a retired middle school teacher. In 1985, when I began teaching German and English to 6th, 7th , 8th, and 9th grade students, I had a sign clearly posted in my classroom. It read: "Your right to be disruptive ends where your classmates' right to a quality education begins."

This concept has application just as much today as it had then. We cannot, and should not, allow the "feelings" of the few, to override the rights of the many. I do not wish to be insensitive, but neither do I wish to be nonsensical. It is biology, not feelings, that determines gender in human beings. We must keep that fact in mind if we wish to avoid the chaos which will disrupt the education of the many. Yes, I have empathy for the girl who feels she is male. That is a struggle no one should have to endure. Yet it is a personal struggle. It is not the obligation of city, county, state, or federal government agencies - or school districts -- to spend taxpayer funds, time, or other resources in an effort to address the "feelings" of those who wish to be another gender.

We live in a time when nonsense prevails. We have five U.S. Supreme Court judges who have twisted the Constitution of the United States into a pretzel. Did these justices not receive a basic education in biology as well as law? Humans are not ovoviviparous. We are not gastropods or other forms of hermaphrodite biological specimens. We are mammals. Placental mammals. Our females nourish their young within the womb. Females have specific reproductive organs. Males have others. The male and female external genital organs differ. Basic biology. As a result of these differences, male-male and female-female sexual union is not natural. It cannot result, for example, in natural birth.

Ah, and there it is. That word "natural." Our courts, our news media, and certain agenda-driven agencies - not to mention the Bruce, or Caitlin, Jenners of the world -- have heaped nonsense upon nonsense until we have blinded ourselves with feelings. We no longer pay heed to the natural. This despite the fact that our very forefathers, those who gave this nation its Constitution, were of such education that they knew, and took into consideration, nature - the natural.

Consider those 56 men I have previously written about in this newspaper. The 56 American founding leaders who wrote about "the Laws of Nature and of Nature's God." These words were part of our Declaration of Independence. It is inconceivable that these men would have been unaware of the basics of biology! I certainly doubt they would have ever imagined a time when our nation would be struggling with such issues as whether a girl should be using a boys' school bathroom, or whether a male should be marrying a male.

Hence I applaud Judge Doumer and county clerk Kim Davis. May they, and many more of us, bring forth sense to a world filled with nonsense. -30-

Dear Representative

I am writing in regard to DoD's recent proposal to increase medical costs for military retirees.

It was my understanding when I joined the USAF in the 1960s that should I serve a full career, medical care would be included in my retirement package.

Now that the Nation finds itself in a severe financial crisis and the DoD budget is under attack, it appears military retiree benefits are the first thing on the chopping block.

The TRICARE fee increases and TRICARE for Life enrollment fees are especially egregious, and then in future years the proposal indexes those fees to medical inflation. A few months ago Congress passed a law stating that fees would not increase any faster than the CoLA increases on retired pay...now already this proposal asks for more from our retirees by linking fees to medical inflation, which has averaged 6.2% over that past two decades.

Please vote your opposition to these healthcare cost increases, as they amount to nothing more than a disproportionate tax increase targeted at a segment of our population that has already given so much to this Nation.

Silence Not Option

Silence is not an option. All too often silence is interpreted as agreement. This is why silence is not an option. I am compelled to speak up even at the risk of being accused - unjustly - of "hate crime." So let me clarify up front: I do not hate atheists, I do not hate homosexuals of either gender, and I do not hate errant political leaders. I do hate evil.

The Random House Dictionary of the English Language, second edition, unabridged - which sits atop a file cabinet next to my desk - offers fourteen individual but related definitions of evil. So, please, do not try to waffle on this. Evil exists. So does good. And just for the record, that same dictionary has 58 entries offering variant definitions of "good." How about that? At least in the dictionary good outweighs evil by a ratio greater than 4:1. I find that interesting, and perhaps hopeful. It is also worth noting that dictionary definitions of both "evil" and "good" involve using such words as moral, immoral, bad, wicked, virtuous, and righteous.

So if you - at this early point - are beginning to feel a bit squeamish, this might be where you choose to bail out. That's fine! Go ahead. It's your choice! Your First Amendment freedom, right? So fine. Bail out. But in doing so, be sure to grant me the same First Amendment right you claim for yourself. I will not be silent. I will talk about evil, and good. And I hope to do so without being or sounding self-righteous. No, I am not a member of the clergy, not in a leadership position in any religion or church. And I am not attempting to persuade you to join or endorse any religious organization. But I am going to talk about atheists and homosexuality and errant political leaders. And, yes, about good and evil.

I'll start by drawing attention to the writings of those we have come to call our country's forefathers. Now I'm not going to do a footnoted doctoral dissertation here. Others have already done so. But let's agree, be you atheist, Christian, or otherwise that George Washington, Thomas Jefferson, and others of the time used the words God, Almighty, and Creator in both official and unofficial writings as our nation was being formed. (Suffice these from the oft quoted Declaration of Independence: the Laws of Nature and of Nature's God .... all men are ... endowed by their Creator .... with a firm reliance on the protection of Divine Providence) and these by Washington who called upon "the Supreme Ruler of the Universe" and "Almighty Being who rules over the universe" and "His divine blessing...." to make the point.

So, whether you are atheist, Christian, or any other, please be honest enough to admit that those who founded our country and developed its system of laws did believe that there is God and that He is Almighty and Creator. The point is: you are free to opt out of such belief. But, you are <u>not</u> free to remove belief in and acknowledgment of God from the legal, political, and social fabric of this nation! We are and will remain "One Nation under God."

Notes worth keeping:

*Comment re positions on pastor-same gender wedding - homosexuality :

It may be legitimate for one to say homosexual behavior - including same-gender marriage – is not a sin, but one must realize that in doing so you may be claiming to be equal to God! For if man judges what is or is not sin, man places self as God's equal. Does not making such a statement deny the truth of God's revealed and inspired Word? In short, if we accept the Bible as the inspired and revealed Word of God then we call God a liar when we contradict Him.

Lev 18
22"'Do not have sexual relations with a man as one does with a woman; that is detestable.

Romans 1
27In the same way the men also abandoned natural relations with women and were inflamed with lust for one another. Men committed shameful acts with other men, and received in themselves the due penalty for their error.
32Although they know God's righteous decree that those who do such things deserve death, they not only continue to do these very things but also approve of those who practice them.
Romans 2
2Now we know that God's judgment against those who do such things is based on truth.
cf. Lev 20:13, 1 Cor 6:9, Jude 1:7, Rom 1:24

Get it Right, George

Your column (of January 9, 2012, Winchester Star) has merit. It would have far greater merit, however, if you would have your research staff provide a bit of salient but absent information. Outgoing Social Security "redistribution" payments are of two categories: some payments go to retirees while other payments go to non-retirees. Writers, like yourself, and many politicians, like Mr. Santorum, too often ignore the distinction.

Here, in brief, is the distinction: retirees worked and paid into the system. Non-retiree recipients are the social beneficiaries of a Congressional revision to the Social Security Plan made some thirty or more years ago. (I don't have a research staff, but my memory points to the Johnson administration or shortly thereafter.) The non-retiree payouts fit rather well into what you, Mr. Will, characterize as "government's redistributive activities." You would be doing your readers a real service if you would offer some truly informative facts regarding the size of the non-retiree payouts, and balance that with facts showing the amounts retirees contributed to the system. With such, your column would have far greater merit.

(Note: I am not reluctant to go up against the "biggies" in the business. When they're wrong, they're wrong. Someone needs to tell them so. George Will is a nationally known and respected syndicated columnist whose work appears in newspapers all around the nation. He also has my respect. When he's right!)

There ought to be

There ought to be a son-in-law appreciation day.

So, now there is!

If every father-in-law were blessed with a clone of this father-in-law's son-in-law then the world we live in would be a so much better place.

Lew, I cannot over-express how much we love you and appreciate you and thank the Lord of Heaven for you.

I've said it before and I'll say it again: There is not a guy on this planet I would rather have by my daughter's side, now, always, and especially when times are difficult.

You have shown your care and your love, your thoughtfulness and your tenderness through some stressful days especially this past year. You have demonstrated the loving and living nature of your vows. What a model you are to your own children! What a priceless partner you are to Iris!

So consider today the official inauguration of Son-in-law Appreciation Day!

Go have a great day of golf at Shenandoah Valley Golf Club!

Take a friend, or Lance, or both!

Congressional embezzlement

Imagine you are the owner of ABC Widget Company and that you have just discovered some of your employees have regularly been leaving company premises during paid work hours. These employees have been collecting pay for work not performed. And while they were away, your widget production fell.

Wouldn't you, as a business owner, feel you have been wronged? Wouldn't you feel you have a legal right to recover your losses?

I'd side with the business owner on this one. Call me old-fashioned, but I was raised in a generation that believed a dollar's worth of work ought to be rendered for a dollar's worth of pay. I'd feel that the business owner ought to legally recover not only the lost wages, but he also should recover his losses for widgets not produced.

Now, fellow Star reader, would you be surprised if I told you that nearly every member of the U.S. Congress is doing precisely what those imaginary wayward employees of ABC Widget Company were doing? Am I saying that your congressman is collecting a $174,000 salary and is leaving company premises during paid work hours? Yes, that is precisely what I am saying. And more. Our elected congressional representatives are pocketing the salary that you and I pay them and are busily "out of their offices" engaged as telemarketers. They are dialing your phone number and mine raising funds for their next election!

There are "call centers" complete with "scripts" to aid individual congressmen in "dialing for dollars." Both parties have told newly elected members of Congress that they "should spend 30-hours a week" in these call centers which are conveniently located just down the street from their offices.

Why just down the street? Because by law members of Congress cannot make such fund-raising calls from their offices. So our elected representatives circumvent the law, go outside of their offices and spend 4 or more hours a day making fund-raising calls. They are literally told to do so by political party leadership. Why? Because the Political Action Committees (PACs and Super-PACs) have helped fund their elections. Congressmen are told their first priority each day is to raise $18,000 to replenish the Super-PAC's funds for the next election.

If you would like to verify this, you can do what I did. Go online to the CBS website and navigate to Season 48, Episode 32 of the 60-Minutes show. You can hear reporter Norah O'Donnell interviewing Florida Rep. (R), David Jolly, Wisconsin Rep. (R) Reid Ribble, New York Rep. (D) Steve Israel, and Minnesota Rep. (D Rick Nolan. You'll hear these congressmen spell out the details. They are sponsoring a bill (H.R. 4443) attempting to stop the practice of federal elected employees from "dialing for dollars."

Rep. Israel admits he has spent more than 4,000 hours soliciting donations. Israel adds that congressmen spend more time raising money than on constituent needs or being on the floor of Congress. Rep. Nolan tells us the "last few years of Congress have been the most unproductive ever."

Now let's return to our imaginary ABC Widget Company. If you or I were among those employees collecting pay for work not performed, would we not likely be prosecuted under the law? Might we not be convicted for embezzlement? Why, then, do we sit idly by and allow our elected congressmen to break the law?

-30-

To his credit

To his credit President-elect Trump, whatever my own misgivings about Trump the man, has already written a positive footnote to election 2016.

He has won as a Washington outsider. He has won without the support of his own party's leadership. He has won without selling his soul to big-ticket political donors. He has won with a campaign financed almost entirely by his own funds.

We should note, factually, that when he used his own facilities to host political events he forfeited the opportunity to book those same facilities for profit-making events. He has won on his platform and policies, not on his personality.

He has won because he studied and learned the election system and its rules.

President-elect Trump can begin his term without catering to special interest groups. He is in a much better position to fulfill his campaign promises than any president-elect I can remember. That's a fresh start I'm eager to see!

-30-

I disagree with a First Lady

Mrs. Obama, I must respectfully but vehemently disagree with you. You have said, "...when we go to the polls this November, the real choice isn't between Democrat or Republican. It's about who will have the power to shape our children...."

Shape our children? No! That is the very last thing I want our federal government to do. I absolutely do not want the 535 members of our Congress to shape my children. Even less do I want the U.S. Department of Education with its 4,300 employees and its $60 billion budget to shape my children.

It is my responsibility and my right as a parent to shape my children. It is the obligation of all parents to "shape their children."

Mrs. Obama - and may I say that I do respect you as First Lady and as a parent - but in that one sentence you have clarified with precision why I and other parents cannot, will not, vote for a continuation of failed and immoral policies. Immoral policies? Yes, immoral! Shall we enumerate? How about the murder of more than one million babies each year. Each year! Oh, the Democrat-Liberal leadership doesn't call it murder. It's abortion. It's disguised as health care for women. It is happening throughout our country because those 535 people we call Congress have legislated in favor of it and our Supreme Court has granted its stamp of approval.

These are the people you propose ought to "shape" my children? Misguided liberals who believe we Americans are incapable of surviving without federal assistance, and pathetic, spineless Republicans who, despite a majority in both Houses of Congress, have forfeited every opportunity to stem the tide, the slide into immorality. I repeat. These are the people you propose ought to "shape" my children? Those same 535 elected legislators are actively promoting the destruction of our nation's families! How? Well, in what dream world does same-gender marriage promote the growth, the health, of families? No, I do not want our Congress, our Supreme Court, or federal bureaucrats to "shape" my children!

I want local schools, local school boards, schools of my choice to be agents of my choice in the shaping of my children. I want private schools, Christian schools, charter schools, and home-schooling as choices I can make to help "shape" my children.

So, thank you, Mrs. Obama. You have made clear my choice for this year's Presidential election. I decidedly do not plan to elect candidates who believe it is their obligation to "shape" my children. Nor will I support a continuation of failed and immoral policies!

--30--

Fiscal shell game

Parents, imagine your dismay if you'd just discovered that with the school lunch money you gave him this morning Johnny had purchased a pornographic magazine rather than pay for his daily nutrition. Chances are you'd feel shocked, betrayed, and convinced it is time for some serious parental intervention. Well, that's just the way I feel right now about a similar scenario, but one of far greater magnitude.

You see, a fiscal shell game involving your tax money and mine is being played right under our noses. It's an "in-your-face" act of deceit and subterfuge. And the only way we can rectify this is with our own "parental intervention" at the polls, November 8.

I'm going to offer you some facts you may not have had, or taken, time to look into. And I will identify my sources if you so request, but this is not a college term paper. No room here for footnotes. But rest assured, I am not making this up. Now to the fiscal shell game and its consequences. Our federal government (think Congress) provides funding (think tax revenue) for Planned Parenthood. Planned Parenthood has just announced it will spend at least $20 million in the 2016 election cycle to help elect the Democratic frontrunner.

So my taxes and yours, fellow reader, are extracted from our paychecks, funneled through Planned Parenthood, and deposited in Hillary Clinton's campaign account. If that is not an "in-your-face" act of deceit and subterfuge, then what is it?

Second, case, with fewer words. When I was a middle school teacher I annually declined to join the National Education Association (NEA). They call themselves "the nation's largest professional employee organization ... committed to advancing the cause of public education." Well, guess what folks. They play the same fiscal shell game as do AARP and Planned Parenthood. Take money for one category, spend it for another.

Third case with still fewer words. I once supported the Susan G. Komen Race for the Cure (dedicated to breast cancer cure.) I stopped my donation when I learned that the Komen organization was granting funds to Planned Parenthood.

So, as we approach November 8 we must make a serious decision. One campaign has pledged to defund Planned Parenthood and has hired Marjorie Dannenfelser as chairwoman of its pro-life coalition. The other plans to continue down the slippery slope of murdering unborn babies, the topic of my next article. Think. Inform yourself. Then vote. And, by the way. Tell Johnny to stop using his lunch money for pornographic magazines.

-30-

Are we to ignore Planned Parenthood's role in the deaths of 58 million aborted babies since 1973? When will we stop deceiving ourselves, stop ignoring reality? Calling an abortion health care is like calling decapitation a weight loss program. We howl and shout at ISIS but we quietly ignore Planned Parenthood.

If we were to ask Cecile Richards, President of Planned Parenthood, about the fiscal shell game, she would find a way to tell us, "Oh, it isn't the federal money we're using to support Mrs. Clinton." To which I would respond, "But without the government's $528 million, you would not be able to contribute $20 million to Hillary." So, what do we know about Cecile Richards? Well, "Before joining Planned Parenthood, Ms. Richards served as deputy chief of staff for House Democratic Leader Nancy Pelosi." That speaks volumes!

You see, fellow readers, I have seen this fiscal shell game before. More than once. Some time ago I was considering whether I should join AARP, the well known retiree services organization. I wrote and asked whether AARP uses member funds to support any particular political candidates or parties. I received a response. No. We do not. Later, I discovered the fiscal shell game. True, AARP itself does not do so. But AARP does route millions of its dollars to the AARP Foundation. This is AARP's affiliated charity. It is this organization that contributes to political candidates and campaigns. That, fellow readers, is a fiscal shell game. Deceit by any other name would smell as rotten, to misquote Shakespeare.

Slippery Slopes

The Hillary people can go ahead and consider me a "mentally deficient" knucklehead from a "basket of deplorables." That's okay with me, because by the time you reach the tail end of this article you'll likely have a different idea as to who best fits into the basket.

Let's begin by addressing the slippery slope of murdering unborn babies. That's a phrase I used in a previous article. I can assure you this: The Democrat-Liberal crowd will object to that terminology. You see, they consider themselves "progressives." And "murdering unborn babies" is not what progressives call abortion. No. Abortion is more comfortably defined as "health care for women." That is a tactic of language manipulation known as a euphemism. The "progressive" party prefers to "use a word or phrase that is more neutral, vague, or indirect to replace a direct, harsh, unpleasant, or offensive term."

But I, too, can play that game. You see, a dictionary tells us that a "progressive" is one who "advocates social, economic, or political reform." That's the comfortable definition. But that same dictionary tells us that "progressive" describes "a disease that becomes more widespread or severe over time."

Which of these definitions do you think best describes those who pursue the agenda of murdering unborn babies?

So, let's examine that slippery slope. You can decide later which definition to apply to our country's Democrat-Liberal-Progressive candidates. The slope begins with an often quoted number of 58 million abortions in the U.S. since 1973. We start the count with 1973 because that was when our Supreme Court legalized abortion. That was 43-years ago. The beginning of the slippery slope.

Now, to be reasonably fair about it, not all of those 1.3 million aborted babies per year can be attributed to the doings of Planned Parenthood. I'm not sure anyone knows the true number one can ascribe to that organization. What we do know is that abortion has become part of the fabric of our society.

Our nation, with the help of Planned Parenthood, didn't stop with routine medical extractions of living human beings.

No, now we have a Clergy Advocacy Board which supports Planned Parenthood "in conversations about women's health." There it is again. Women's health. No concern for the rights, let alone the comfort, of the baby! But thanks to the Clergy Advocacy Board we have conversations like this:

"*A Presbyterian minister in my city once said that he would support his teenage daughter to get an abortion. When another pastor asked him, "When do you believe a human person begins to exist?" The Presbyterian minister replied, "I think someone becomes a person when they are loved."*

That's part of the slippery slope. But so is this. Here is a recent Planned Parenthood announcement: "We are thrilled to announce we will begin offering appointments for transgender hormone provision at all of our health centers." If you know what this has to do with planning for parenthood, please share your knowledge with me.
One further concern. How long will it be before we in this country begin doing what is already being done in Europe? Belgium has legalized euthanasia for children between the ages of 1 to 12. Please notice this:

The Dutch Health Minister, Edith Schippers, has earmarked almost 400,000 Euros for a study of whether to expand eligibility for euthanasia to children between 1 and 12. At the moment, children under 1 may be killed with the consent of their parents. After neighboring Belgium passed legislation in 2014 enabling child euthanasia, doctors and activists in the Netherlands are keen to catch up.

And over in Northern Ireland folks are debating this:

The truth is that Mick Wallace's abortion bill seeks to establish a new era of discrimination where babies with severe disabilities can be legally considered as less than human, and not entitled to the full protection of the law.

So how long will it be until we hear this conversation in America?

11-year-old Susie: "Mom, why are you tossing my laptop into that cardboard box?"

4-year-old Seth: “Mom, why are you tossing my teddy bear into that cardboard box?”
Mom to both: “You won’t be needing it. Tomorrow you’ll be euthanized.”

Readers, please vote on November 8. Yes, even those of us who are “mentally deficient deplorables in a basket.”

-30-

My Thoughts on Their Thoughts

Krauthammer writes: "The Affordable Care Act.... is amended at will by presidential fiat." (Feb 13, 2014).

My Thoughts: This is yet another Case (I will elaborate below) of President Obama violating the law, the very Constitution he swore an oath to defend. How is he violating the Constitution you ask? Well, let's take a peek at the document he swore to defend.
Quote:
Article. I.
Section. 1.
All legislative Powers herein granted shall be vested in a Congress of the United States, which shall consist of a Senate and House of Representatives.

So, for starters, amending a law is a legislative act. But the Constitution grants "all legislative powers" to the Congress.

So when a President, such as Obama, amends a law, he is taking upon himself the powers granted to the Congress. It is the Congress, and only the Congress which can amend a law.

You see, this nation's forefathers had experienced firsthand what happens when too much power is in the hands of a single person, or a single agency. That is why they designed our government (by means of the Constitution) featuring a balance of powers.

I should be surprised that our current President does not know, or does not choose to know, this very basic "balance of powers" feature of the Constitution. After all, every American high school student must study this very information prior to graduation! Surely our current President is a high school graduate! Isn't he?

Now the part of the Constitution that specifies the duties and responsibilities of the President is this:
Quote:
Article. II.
Section. 1.
The executive Power shall be vested in a President of the United States of America ....

--30--

(Here I go again, going up against the biggies. Krauthammer, whom I do respect, like George Will, is a nationally syndicated columnist.)

A sense of purpose

One waxes ever more eloquently as that sixth decade of life approaches, eh? This is as it ought to be. Time. Distance. These are ingredients of the seasoning of reasoning. Looking back. Peering ahead. With a bit more squint in the eyes than once was the case. Ah, the pondering. I, too, wonder at the sense of purpose, the productivity of times past. Yet my wonderment reaches back to times of wooden, creaking, bone-jarring, canvas-covered vehicles. The time between the quest of Lewis and Clark and those steel rails that linked the Atlantic to the Pacific.

Yes, today's America seems adrift. Is adrift. And yet. I remember the story of the starfish. (See below if you don't recall that one.) As you peer ahead and contemplate the meaning, the value, of your own "grain of sand" in the castle of dreams, remember this. Today's world has a map. Someone made it possible to find a way to unscramble the recipes of life itself. That "someone" created a device capable of reading encoded letters of the alphabet, the script of life. Others applied this "discovery" with results such as these.

- The Human Genome Project has already fueled the discovery of more than 1,800 disease genes.

- As a result of the Human Genome Project, today's researchers can find a gene suspected of causing an inherited disease in a matter of days, rather than the years it took before the genome sequence was in hand.

- There are now more than 2,000 genetic tests for human conditions. These tests enable patients to learn their genetic risks for disease and also help healthcare professionals to diagnose disease.

- At least 350 biotechnology-based products resulting from the Human Genome Project are currently in clinical trials.

You and I, son, have this in common (among other things, I'd guess). Much of the work **we** do in the background, behind the scenes, has permitted others -- those with "connections" or with "funding" or with "notoriety" - to bring to fruition that which **we** have conceived. Similarly, our work in the field of education. You with your understanding and application of technology, and I with classroom application of the best of teaching techniques, have touched minds.

We may never see the results. But there are minds we have nurtured. Some will achieve! Some will venture into realms we never imagined! These are the starfish. You have yours. I have mine. Do not lose sight of these presently invisible results.

As for the starfish, I recall, during one of those otherwise interminable "teacher improvement" seminars, this little anecdote:

> *A young man walked up a shore littered with thousands of starfish, beached and dying after a storm. An old man was picking them up and flinging them back into the ocean. "Why do you bother?" the young man scoffed. "You're not saving enough to make a difference." The old man picked up another starfish and sent it spinning back to the water. "Made a difference to that one," he said.*

As I said. You have yours. I have mine. Starfish, that is.

-30-

What? YouTube Valuable?

Yes, Lance, ----food for thought. But do you know what he left out? He listed (some) other countries which are free. He mentioned Japan, United Kingdom (U.K.), France, Italy, Germany, Belgium, Spain, and Australia. He could have added Netherlands, Denmark, Greece, Turkey -- and several others. And do you -- Lance -- know why those countries are free? I'll tell you what he -- the speaker -- did not. Those countries (and others not mentioned) are "free" because of the blood of American soldiers spilled on the soils of those countries!!!!

Go to the (still existing today) American cemeteries in France, Luxembourg, Belgium and other countries, and you will see (as I have) the graves of thousands of Americans! These were soldiers! American soldiers! Row after row after row of crosses, headstones, of Americans buried in places thousands of miles from their homes in Ohio, Kansas, New Jersey, and many other states. These were young men who died on foreign soil. That is why those countries (mentioned by the speaker) are free!!!

Were it not for the blood spilled by Americans (and, yes, the other Allies), Hitler and Hirohito would have been successful in their quests for imperial world control. Freedom would not exist, and we would all be speaking (involuntarily) either Japanese or German.

That is what the speaker neglected to tell you. You, however, Lance, are more fortunate than the blond co-ed that the speaker excoriated. You have two living grandfathers and one living father who know why those countries are free!

And, yes! America is not the greatest country in the world anymore! For the very reasons the YouTube speaker cited! We are no longer "informed" because we choose to focus far too much of our attention upon the frivolous!

So, yes, for the reasons he mentioned, we have forfeited our right to call ourselves the greatest nation!

Your generation -- if it so chooses -- could restore that greatness!

--Thoughts from your Virginnygramps!

-30-

On Scientology

Lance, I was hurrying out the door as I jotted a response to your question about Scientology. Had I had another moment, I'd have added this: The goal of professed Scientologists is to become a "thetan."

This word is comprised of a prefix deriving from the Greek word *theos* meaning god (you'll recall the Latin *deus.* Same word.). The suffix *an* expresses the meaning "*one who is.*" Words like human or Texan come to mind here.

Now, the problem with the Scientologists seeking to become a thetan is, as I referenced earlier, that it equates man with God. And Lance, if there is anything that man is not capable of being, it is that of being God!

History is replete with examples of haughty humans who believed themselves to be god, a god, or God. Do some research, and you'll learn what became of both men and nations who held such beliefs. (Hint: thumb through some history books. See if you can find some empires once existing but no longer existing today.)

You, Lance, are a product of the Judeo-Christian culture into which you were born. Before one rejects one's heritage, should such ever occur to you, one ought first know thoroughly what that culture truly is.

I envy your current time of scholarly exploration! And I fully encourage you to gain all that you can from it. And yes, that includes exploration of what colleges of my time called *Religions of the World.* I studied them, too. And I chose to hold fast to the Judeo-Christian culture of which I am part.

p.s. Scientology is not part of that Judeo-Christian culture. And please note what I am not saying here. I am not saying Scientologists are evil people. Some may be. Some not. I am saying I am not interested in what they have to offer.

2nd p.s. The brochure I gave your mom last evening is for you to peruse. It is a useful capsule comparison of key features of a dozen or so religious beliefs.

That said, remember what I said to you many months ago. God is. It's up to you to deal with that fact.

-30-

On Love

Lance, I sense this may be an opportune time for me to offer some discerning thoughts on the topic of love. And, I hope you will see as we progress here, that my offering is of little if any value if you are unwilling to receive that which is offered. So my greatest hope at the moment is that you are both receptive and willing to receive. Granted, this will sound a bit formal - sort of a discourse, or an essay - and that is so because the topic, if we are to avoid the frivolous, demands a bit of formality. That said, the topic is that of the giving and receiving of love. Now, if you reflect on it, you will recognize that this is a topic about which your parents and your two sets of grandparents have a bit of experience.

Notice that I did not say that we are experts on the matter. We, as so with any human beings, have from time to time erred and allowed some of the prime ingredients of the process to get out of balance. Key word there was "process" for love is just that. It is an ongoing process. Keep that at the forefront of your mind as we progress here. Let's start with "gift giving." This is an easy introduction, because your mother has done such a wonderful job of modeling this for you and teaching you how to add value to the event. Think of any gift-giving occasion. Birthday, Christmas, anniversary. One person offers a gift, and another receives.

If you, the recipient, hurriedly and thoughtlessly shove the gift off to the side and move on to more immediate things, you would wound the gift-giver. If you later toss the gift up upon the closet shelf and never so much as open it, you would add distress to the gift-giver's wound. Over the years, your mother has modeled and taught you how to lovingly complete the cycle of the gift-giving event. First you read and share the card, right? You express thanks. Then you somewhat ceremoniously grasp and unwrap the gift. Sounds, smiles, comments expressing appreciation then follow. You might hold the gift up for others to see. You might make comment about how the gift-giver knew just the right gift for you. Again, you publicly thank the gift-giver. Sometimes with a hug and a kiss. At some time in the future you make a special effort to model or use the gift in the presence of the gift-giver. That cycle of the gift-giving process is, in fact, very much like the process of love experienced between two people. Again, note the word "process."

You see, Lance, love is a process. It is an ongoing and ever-growing process. And like the gift-giving scenario, love is not complete without reciprocity. Without reciprocity, love wounds, withers, and dies. Just days ago, Lance, I learned something new (new, that is, to me) and for that new knowledge I have your Latin lessons to thank. I'll return to that. But for now let's continue with the thread.

The reciprocity of love is like an oval. The giving is complete only with the receiving. The receiving responds with giving. The giver becomes the recipient who again becomes the giver. From this, it is clear that love is "other-directed." And this is the distinction between love and self-satisfaction. From this, you can perceive that the pursuit of self-satisfaction interrupts the cyclical nature of love. There can be no reciprocity when self-satisfaction is the goal. This is true also, Lance, in the physical realm. Physical intimacy is an ingredient of love, or an expression of love. And as with the "process" of love, physical intimacy relies upon that same "other-directed" nature of love. When the emphasis is upon self-satisfaction rather than mutual-satisfaction, the cycle of reciprocity is interrupted and love falters.

Now Lance, you are "of" and "at" an age where you are naturally desiring and seeking expressions of love. It is of lasting importance to you that you take the time, apply your intellect, and make distinctions between matters of the heart, matters of the physical intimacy, and matters of the process and cycle of love.

If, on balance, a person with whom you establish a friendship, or a deeper relationship, exhibits a series of behaviors which tend toward "self-interest" or "self-satisfaction" to a greater degree than "other-directed" love, then you might want to reassess the relationship. You might argue that people change. I would agree. But to this I would add that such change may be many years in forthcoming, and "change" might also include changing to greater degrees of what presently exists. You, Lance, must envision, to the best of your ability, whether the seeds of a present relationship will grow into a pear tree or into a prickly-pear cactus.

Now let me return to something I recently learned thanks to our joint-venture Latin lessons. As you know, I have been engaged in pursuit of greater knowledge of and love of God through study of Scripture. In the process, I've come across some ideas about love, and about "perfect" love. Now please do not erect a mental barrier here. I spent far too much of my life doing just that (erecting barriers) only to discover the obvious: barriers separate. Bridges connect.

Shortly I will return to the word "perfect," but first let's focus on the word "love."

"Love is patient, love is kind and is not jealous; love does not brag and is not arrogant, does not act unbecomingly; it does not seek its own, is not provoked, does not take into account a wrong suffered, does not rejoice in unrighteousness, but rejoices with the truth; bears all things, believes all things, hopes all things, endures all things. Love never fails ...."

These thoughts come from the Apostle Paul and are found in 1 Corinthians 13:4. They express many of the characteristics of love. Note in particular that phrase, "does not seek its own." To complete that thought, add the word "satisfaction."

Now let's return to the word "perfect." In my Biblical studies I came across these:

2Cor13:11 Finally, brothers, farewell. Be perfect ....

Col1:28 that we may present every man perfect in Christ;

And

1John4:17 By this, love is perfected with us, so that we may have confidence in the day of judgment; because as He is, so also are we in this world.

Just weeks ago, I had a major "eye-opener" regarding these and similar Biblical phrases. I had thought the meaning of "perfect" to be that of "without fault" or "without blemish."

And this troubled me because it seemed that Biblical authors were urging us (mankind) to be what only God can be. The logical outcome of this thinking is that man can be as perfect as God. And that, of course, would make God and man equal, or at least capable of being equal. I knew in my heart that such could not be the case, but there it was in the Bible.

Enter Latin. And grammar. You know, despite the fact that I am well educated in English grammar, German grammar, and Latin grammar, I never had taken the time to dwell on why it was we called past-tense verbs "perfect." Perfect tense. Most often my brain inquires "why" – why is this or that so? In this case I just blew right past it. Never really gave it a second thought. If I had done so (as now I have done so) I would have been a better teacher. I could have clarified for my students that the word "perfect" itself derives from a Latin word expressing "complete." So the grammar term "perfect tense" expresses an action which is or has become "complete." As in "finished." And this has nothing to do with error-free or without blemish.

So now, Lance, what does this have to do with our topic, "love"? Just this. Perfect love does not mean love without blemish, it means love which is complete.

And that brings us back to our starting point -- the giving and receiving of love. Reciprocity is an act of completion.

So as you reflect upon the nature of a loving relationship, you will find yourself better able to ascertain the merits of your current or any future relationship. If a partner exhibits greater self-interest than "other-interest" then the process of love is highly likely to wither and cause agony and pain. And those might last a lifetime.

-30-

Two words

A clear understanding of the difference between two words could quench flames of discord presently searing the very fabric of our nation. Examples of our discord abound.

Why the friction? Well, often the catalyst is our focus upon "my rights" which tends to cloud any recognition of "your rights" not to mention "our rights."

The two words? Consider these: allow and compel. If we'd take the time to consider distinctions between these two words, not every spark would launch a forest fire.

For example, on the topic of same-sex marriage, a law allowing two males or two females to marry one another need not compel a county clerk, a pastor, a priest, or a rabbi to participate in that marriage. A same-gender couple while respectfully recognizing the rights of others retains the option to seek out another official whose conscience, or faith, does allow such participation.

And how does this differ from racial discrimination? The matter of same-sex marriage is a choice. The matter of race is not. This is why a baker ought <u>not</u> be compelled to bake a wedding cake nor a seamstress to design a wedding gown if they cannot in good conscience participate in a same-sex marriage. The couple is free to seek out another baker, another seamstress. Again, this is not the same as racial discrimination.

The views of John G. Roberts, Jr., Chief Justice of the U.S. Supreme Court are instructive here. He wrote in his June 26, 2015 dissenting opinion in Obergefell v. Hodges: "Unlike criminal laws ... the marriage laws at issue here involve no government intrusion. They create no crime and impose no punishment. Same-sex couples remain free to live together, to engage in intimate conduct, and to raise their families as they see fit."

The Chief Justice also lambasted his fellow judges saying, "But as a judge, I find the majority's position indefensible as a matter of constitutional law... Allowing unelected federal judges to select which unenumerated rights rank as 'fundamental'–and to strike down state laws on the basis of that determination–raises obvious concerns about the judicial role."

So, it seems even our highest court fails, at times, to make the distinction between allow and compel. And they are not alone in this regard. Many who call themselves Christians make the same error. Some need to apply the Paul Harvey ("the rest of the story") technique when they read their Bibles. One needs to read not only carefully selected snippets but rather entire chapters. Only then will Christians come to recognize that, yes, Leviticus 18 clearly states that "You shall not lie with mankind, as with womankind: it is abomination..." but Romans 1 completes the story in Paul Harvey fashion by adding, "Therefore God also gave them up to uncleanness through the lusts of their own hearts, to dishonor their own bodies between themselves."

And there it is. The distinction between those two words. God allows but does not compel. He gives each of us the freedom to choose, even when by that choice one is opting to condemn oneself.

Of course our courts must protect the interests of society. It is one thing to harm oneself. Quite another to harm someone else. This returns us to our nation in discord. Yes, per the first Amendment to our Constitution we have the right to "assemble, and to petition the Government." But we must not ignore the word "peaceably" which precedes both assemble and petition."

This brings us to Ferguson, Missouri, and to a second connotation for allow and compel. Someone forgot to allow the facts to precede the compelling of action. Thomas Sowell, a black columnist, understood this distinction when he wrote of the, "demonstrable lie that Michael Brown was shot in the back by a white policeman in Missouri."

Unlike the crowds in the streets – out of which was spawned "Black Lives Matter" -- Sowell allowed the facts to demolish the lie while rioters in the streets compelled society to ignite the flames of passion. This not to suggest that we have not experienced egregious examples of police errors, indeed crimes, against black victims. But Ferguson was not one of those.

Too late we see that some want to legitimize that which is illegitimate, some want to act without regard for our Constitution and without regard to the rights of others, and all suffer when we fail to make the distinction between allow and compel.

-30-

On Marriage

How can any U. S. court find a ban on same-gender marriage to be unconstitutional given that neither the word "marriage" nor even the concept of marriage are to be found written in the Constitution?

The clear evidence, then, is that marriage is not an event over which the federal government has any jurisdiction. Marriage is and remains a spiritually-based sacrament involving a life-long covenant between one man and one woman. Hence, the only part of the U.S. Constitution that applies is this: Amendment I. *Congress shall make no law respecting an establishment of religion, or prohibiting the free exercise thereof.*

As to same-gender marriage, that is a matter to be decided at the local level and solely by the participating parties, including, if so desired, any ecclesiastical participation. As for Christians who wish be judgmental on the issue, you need to review John 6:66 and remember that Jesus did not call them back.

And as for same-gender couples, you need to remember that the absence of language within the Constitution is not an accident. Some things are meant to be accomplished at the local level.

So why are we willing to sit and yawn while three Federal District Judges ram their personal social agenda down the throats of Virginia voters who have voted by a margin of 57-43 to retain marriage as a one-man one-woman covenant?

On the Conundrum of Doing One's Best

What youthful person has not had ears filled with exhortations from parents, coaches, teachers, and, oh yes, Uncle Jack. The exhortations? "Do your best!"

Alas! It seems so obvious. Yet youth would oft prefer to "Do the least!" After all, what's the point of filling the blanks on some lifeless worksheet?

No argument there. But, of course, that worksheet sheds more light upon the teacher than upon the point of doing one's best. Still, doing one's best can have deleterious consequences, some as deadly as a rattlesnake's venom. And that toxin is just as likely to spit forth from family, friend, fellow student, or flaccid featherbedding co-worker.

Let's examine first that flaccid featherbedding co-worker. These are your fellow associates, your colleagues. And the work habits they exhibit are the same whether on the "widget" production line or out felling trees for lumber. If you set about to do your best, these folks will resent you. Sometimes to the point of downright hatred. You see, if you produce more widgets than they do, this makes them look bad. They appear not to be performing up to snuff. This same is true whether you're splitting firewood or securing contracts for the production of widget parts.

These flaccid featherbedders are easy to spot, especially where there are unions. Unions encourage doing just enough for the simple reason that that will eventually force the business enterprise to hire more workers. And more workers pay more union dues. But they do not necessarily produce more widgets. What this does for the business enterprise is decrease productivity. It increases the cost of producing the same number of widgets.

So, when you are out there doing your best, and your colleagues are out there doing their least, it won't be long before some of those colleagues find some way to sabotage you.

This same syndrome is a part of your daily life in the classroom. If your sterling performance causes your fellow classmates to either work harder or receive lower grades, you become the target. What "achiever" has not heard the mumbles? Or worse?

So there you are with parents, coaches, teachers, and, oh yes, Uncle Jack, encouraging you to do your best, while friends, classmates, and fellow workers are simultaneously dissuading you. Where might you look for a resolution to this conundrum? Well, for starters you'd do well to recognize that you are neither the first nor alone in facing such treachery.

Consider:

I am the utter contempt of my neighbors
and an object of dread to my closest friends—
those who see me on the street flee from me.
I am forgotten as though I were dead;
I have become like broken pottery.
For I hear many whispering,
"Terror on every side!"
They conspire against me
and plot to take my life.

And this:

I hear many whispering,
"Terror on every side!
Denounce him! Let's denounce him!"
All my friends
are waiting for me to slip, saying,
"Perhaps he will be deceived;
then we will prevail over him
and take our revenge on him."

And these:

Those who want to kill me set their traps,
those who would harm me talk of my ruin;
all day long they scheme and lie.

Because of the voice of the enemy,
because of the oppression of the wicked:
for they cast iniquity upon me,
and in wrath they hate me.

For behold, they lie in wait for my life; fierce men stir up strife against me. For no transgression or sin of mine, O LORD,

The wicked band together against the righteous and condemn the innocent to death.

Yes, these are excerpts from the Bible. You see, the problem of doing well is as old as Scripture itself. Doing one's best amidst people who would rather continue the way of mediocrity is ageless. By the way, the first of these is from Psalm 31 and the second is from Jeremiah 20. The others are from various Psalms.

So what about it? Ought one succumb to the crowd, the clique, the throng? Surely that would be easier than at all times doing one's best. Well, perhaps. But let's consider the flip side of the coin. What might be - and all too often are – the consequences of doing just enough to get by.

Consider:

The engineer who designed the bridge you transit each day ....
The pilot at the controls of your flight to Phoenix....
The nurse who carries out your doctor's orders....
The pharmaceutical researcher who formulates your medicine....
The judge who adjudicates your "life sentence" case....

Do you really want these to be the "just do the minimum" kind of people?

Get real! We'd still be living the life of Fred Flintstone if the "just enough" folks had their way!

We advanced from the first powered flight in 1903 to spaceflight and walking upon the moon in 1969! That was not done by the "let's do the least" crew.

In combat, do you want the "just enough" guy on your right?

In the classroom do you want the "do the minimum" teacher to prepare you?

In food preparation, do you want the "okay, that's good enough" for kitchen clean-up?

Enough said, right? We have established that the "do your best" approach can, and often does, result in you being on the receiving end of the enmity of the bone-head portion of the population. But, we have also established that the "doing just enough" method will result in anything from mediocrity to death!

Decide!

-30-

On the Word "No!"

This applies to both parties, both houses of Congress and to all elected officials:

"No!" You are not self-employed! I, the American voter, am your boss and your supervisor!
"No!" Your first priority is NOT your own re-election!
"No!" It is NOT okay to misspend taxpayer money on yourself, your family, or your friends!
"No!" It is NOT okay for you to receive any pension beyond a self-purchased plan!
"No!" It is NOT okay for you to exempt yourself from contributing to Social Security!
"No!" It is NOT okay for you to accept any government-provided healthcare benefit beyond the Tricare you provide for our military forces!
"No!" It is NOT okay for you to slip "pork" (or, "earmark") amendments into any other piece of legislation. If it's worth voting for, it stands alone, on its own merit!
"No!" It is NOT okay for you to propose or vote upon on any legislative measure or measures which require expenditure of funds greater than the previous year's revenues. In brief: this year's spending must never exceed last year's revenue.
"No!" It is NOT okay for you to burden the next generation with this generation's debt!
"No!" It is NOT okay for you to use time, funds, vehicles, computers, or any other resources of the government for any purpose other than accomplishing the legitimate work of the government!
"No!" It is NOT okay to accept money, vacations, or gifts from lobbyists or anyone else who is seeking largesse,

benefits, or contracts from the federal government, or to propose or vote-upon any legislative measure which benefits your financial holdings, your business, your friends' businesses, or the businesses of any of your family members!

"No!" It is NOT okay for you to ignore, to expunge, or to relegate to the trash-bin the very Judeo-Christian values which this nation's forefathers specifically included in their deliberations and within the documents which founded this nation!

Yes! You must abide by the Constitution you promised by "oath" to support and defend!

And, "Yes" I will use that same Constitution to vote you out of office. That's why I do not need to add "term limits" to the Constitution. I already have the right to terminate your employment!

Open Letter to Mr. Trump

Sir, I'm addressing this to you only because at the moment you lead the pack. Lose that lead and this letter goes to the next in line for the Republican nomination.

I am but one voter. I claim no following. But, discard my plea at your own peril. For I am many. I will limit my "wish list" to four items. These are: fair tax, balanced budget, a leader who listens, and, oh yes, unfettered honesty.

Tax. I want what some call fair tax, others call consumer-based tax, value added tax, or tithing. The short of it is that all Federal tax is to be collected at the cash register. Every retail sale, be it the rich man's Maserati or the average man's Chevy, is taxed at the same rate for all. If adopted, this one-stop tax would eliminate the need for the IRS and all of its staff. Why? No forms. No filing deadlines. No investigations. None of that would be needed. Imagine the savings!

Your current tax plan, what little of it you have divulged, is nothing more than the same shell game we have seen for decades. Each time we redefine rich, poor, corporation, or individual, we create loopholes and exclusions. Your proposal (seen on 60-Minutes this past Sunday) offers nothing new.

Hence my support for "fair" tax. Everyone pays at the cash register. Of key importance, everyone pays. Everyone! This overcomes both fact and perception that some -- at both ends of the economic scale -- do not pay, or do not pay enough. Purchase big, pay big. That's fair. Purchase small, pay small. No loopholes, no exclusions, no deductions. This is the tax reform I want the next President to bring to reality.

Balanced budget. It takes only twelve words. And no, I am not oversimplifying. Former Virginia Senator Harry F. Byrd Jr. gave us these twelve words in 1978: “total budget outlays of the Federal Government shall not exceed its receipts." The House passed the bill. The Senate passed the bill. The President signed the bill. So where is it now? Well, it went the way of our country's will. Do the research and you will find what I found. We all know the result of its demise. So, Mr. Candidate (or Ms. Candidate) do what Senator Byrd did. Write, pass, and sign those twelve words. But this time let’s stick with it.

On listening. I want a President who listens to the people of this country. And, as I used to tell my teenagers, the difference between "hearing" and "listening" is action!

Finally, let’s talk about honesty. You, Mr. Trump (again, on 60 minutes) told us you favor honesty. You value honesty. But when asked (during the debate) whether you had filed bankruptcy, you responded, “No.” You gave what I call a “Clinton” style diversion. That’s not honesty. You know full well what the question was. You chose to answer on the basis of individual filing rather than corporate filing. Again, that’s not honesty. If you wish to garner my vote, you must do better than that.

So, yes, I am but one voter. And fair tax, balanced budget, a leader who listens, and, oh yes, unfettered honesty are what I want our next President to deliver. Step aside if you choose not to listen.

-30-

On Being "Qualified"

Thank you, Onofrio Castiglia, for you have exposed the truth! You have given your readers the most clearly articulated statements to date revealing the heart, the soul, the reason-for-being, of the Democrat-Liberal-Progressive movement.

Thanks also to Virginia Governor Terry McAuliffe for peeling the skin away from the onion. This is one time I won't shed tears over peeled onions!

Castiglia's story (Star, March 29) was headlined, "Governor vetoes bill to review applicants for public assistance." He was writing about State House Bill 2092, introduced by Del. Dave LaRock, R-Hamilton.

What was the essence of the bill? Only this: that we voter-taxpayers ought to expect that applicants for public assistance do, in fact, qualify for that assistance. Is the applicant really who he claims to be? We should reasonably expect a routine check of such things as identity (birth records, death records), income, assets, and, oh yes, correctional status.

Why would a Democrat-Liberal-Progressive office holder not want such verification? Here is my one-word answer: accountability! I'll explain below.

But first let's hear what LaRock had to say about the now-vetoed bill. He called the bill a "common-sense anti-fraud initiative." The bill would "ensure that all individuals applying for welfare benefits qualify" for those benefits. He added, "Other states where this effort has been made (have) exposed a significant number of ineligible enrollees." He mentions a 2010 Illinois audit of that state's Medicaid program that "found over 14,000 deceased people on Medicaid rolls."

So, imagine that! LaRock wants folks to be verified, to qualify, before receiving funds which flow from your pocket and mine into theirs. The only flaw with LaRock's proposal is that it falls woefully short of addressing the full scope of the problem. I would argue that we taxpaying voters must demand such verification from recipients of every Federal and every State "benefit" program. Social Security disability benefits alone, if fully audited, would surely reap returns sufficient to put a real dent in the national debt.

We should not doubt the reality of such fraud. Castiglia's report reveals one such case which is, without a doubt, a model for countless others. "An Arlington woman (was) recently arrested on charges of welfare fraud after allegedly collecting more than $100,000 in benefits while her husband was earning $1.5 million per year as an attorney."

So I reasonably ask what Castiglia did not ask of Governor McAuliffe. Why would a Democrat-Liberal-Progressive governor veto such a "common-sense" bill? The answer is accountability!

How many more examples do we taxpaying voters need? The Democrat-Liberal-Progressive movement <u>does not want accountability</u>. What they want is unfettered flow of taxpayer funds to go to those who are most likely to vote in favor of continuation of such government largesse.

So, thank you, Governor, for peeling that onion! As for me, I want accountability for every nickel you and your Democrat-Liberal-Progressive colleagues take from me and give to “unqualifieds.”

-30-

On Balance

Those founding fathers who crafted our Constitution were brilliant! But if they came up short on anything, it was in anticipating man's capacity for corruption. And what we have most recently corrupted (we includes you and I without regard to political party affiliation) is the ever so essential balance of power concept the founders built into that Constitution.

No surprise that our forebears settled on three branches of government. After all, they had just gone "all in" to use today's term. They had ousted the King whose iron grip had encompassed all three functions of government. There was nothing to "balance" the King's power.

Our Constitution, therefore, was fashioned with a legislative, an executive, and a judicial branch. Sure. We've all known this since the 8th grade. But if we have known this, why have we sat idly by and allowed our "leaders" to corrupt our Constitution?

Article III, for example, establishes the Supreme Court and defines its judicial power. But nowhere within that article or any of its subsections do we see language describing what we have recently seen. We have allowed a solitary judge of one subordinate sub-section of the Supreme Court to usurp the power of the President, the Executive Branch.

I challenge you, readers, to find me in error here! Go ahead. Read the entire Constitution and show me where our founding fathers established such judicial power! Yet, in recent months we have seen individual federal judges claim to themselves this power! (Washington state, Hawaii, and New York to name but a few.)

If the U. S. Supreme Court were to halt Executive Branch action, that would demonstrate "balance of power." But for a solitary judge at some distant district to do so, that is judicial tyranny!

Now let's shift our focus to the Congress. Established by our Constitution's Article I, the Congress acts within its "balance of power" when the House and the Senate write and pass proposed bills of law to the President. Such is the power of the Congress.

But we have witnessed, and again idly sat by, as individuals and sub-groups within Congress corrupt the process. The Constitution allows and obligates the Congress to raise and appropriate revenue. This "revenue" is what is required to fund all branches of government so that each can fulfill its obligations to the public. Sounds straightforward, right?

It could be. But some members of Congress have found ways to usurp the process. They do so by not passing appropriation bills on an annual basis, but rather in segments of "continuing resolutions." Then they attempt to tie non-appropriations legislation to the funding bills. We've just seen governmental shutdown owing to this very tactic. That's not "balance of power." That's legislative tyranny!

So that's how we thank those who gave us our Constitution? We have permitted, even encouraged, judicial tyranny and legislative tyranny. That's not party politics. That's absurdity.

It's time for action. Vote!

-30-

Questions the media does not ask

If we wish to address the truly salient issue of the day, we would be asking – make that demanding – the questions our "media" reps do not ask! Why don't we hear the most important questions?

In the interest of transparency, let me state up front: I support none of the current slate of candidates of either party in their quests for the office of President.

Let's start with the most recent "debate" among Republican candidates (March 3, 2016). Media moderators failed (this time) in their early attempt to rankle the candidates into a rash of name-calling. So they had to settle on jibes about the size of hands and other body parts before moving to more legitimate questions.

But once they moved to more substantive questions, why did they use "graphics" to ask only one candidate questions related to budget proposals? Why not ask other candidates that same question? (I'll let that hang there for the moment.)

Later, when Trump was asked about his campaign donations to Democratic candidates in previous election years, he responded forthrightly that he had done so. But when he added "...actually it was for business..." why did no one ask "why" he had made campaign donations "for business"? Might that not have opened the door to asking other candidates why they <u>accept</u> donations from businesses? And might that have led to asking questions regarding legislation governing political campaign donations? And might that have led to revealing that the Constitution of the United States does not so much as address that topic. And might that have led to identifying the Congress itself as the source of legislation governing campaign donations? And might that have led to asking some very relevant questions? Like why do we hire coyotes to guard the chicken ranch?

But, you see, our media reps do not wish to ask such questions. Might that be because so many media reps are not interested in pursuing truth? Might they rather be pursuing advertising revenue (which is based upon television viewer ratings)? And might that explain why they did not address the same graphic-supported budget questions to candidates other than Trump?

How long are we viewers, we the public, going to sit idly by while our media reps pursue a carrion banquet designed only to attract the buzzards which attract the "ratings"?

Would our media reps rather pursue their own agendas of shredding one candidate while promoting another? Okay, that's a rhetorical question. But the fact is our media reps leave us starving for factual, truthful, information while they go willy-nilly their own direction in pursuit of ratings which benefit little more than their own careers. The crowds supporting Trump are not fooled by media sleight of hand. Nor are they unaware of the rot within the halls of Congress. So, here, for the media reps are questions you will probably choose to ignore. How many lobbyist organizations occupy office buildings within a 50-mile radius of Washington D.C.? How many pieces of legislation purportedly proposed by members of Congress during the past 25 or so years were actually written by lobbyists then given to legislators? How many members of Congress have received campaign donations from these lobbyist organizations?

Essentially, these, too, are rhetorical questions. They are questions the media does not ask, and they are questions our government leaders do not wish to answer. But these questions, and many others like them, are what are fueling the interest of the "disenchanted" electorate swelling the rallies and creating the lines at this year's primary elections. Wake up, media reps! Start asking relevant questions!

-30-

On LGBT issues

A public school is a taxpayer funded facility; it is an institution civil government. A Target store is a commercial business; it is not an agency of civil government. We need to remember such factual details as we contemplate issues like the LGBT topic addressed by Mark Anderson (Star, April 27) who, in turn, was responding to a Delegate LaRock letter. And, no, the Anderson letter did not specifically address Target stores. For that I'm drawing upon other media reports.

Let's take a step back and look at the larger picture here. There is widespread confusion and an equal amount of ignorance surrounding LGBT issue. I am a pragmatic sort of person, and I tend to favor reason over emotion.

There is much to agree with in the Anderson letter. For starters I fully agree with this: "Let society dish out punishment on bigotry by refusal to patronize businesses that refuse service based on race, sex, orientation, religion, etc." Please note the emphasis on society here and not government.

Hence, if Target wishes to risk inviting a male predator into a female restroom facility, it has the right to do so. But with that right comes the "rights of others" to cease shopping at Target and the "rights of others" to sue Target given its legal liability for damages that might occur to a female victim sexually assaulted while using a store-owned restroom facility. Of course, my pragmatic nature would ask why Target would not consider installing unisex bathroom chambers. Conflict avoided. Litigation avoided. It is a marketing question, is it not? Why would Target wish to appease the "feelings" of the 100 at the expense of losing the 1,000? Soon enough the commercial results of such a decision will become evident. One business' loss becomes another's gain.

In like fashion, if an entertainer chooses not to perform in one location or another, he has that right. Just as I have the right not to attend his performances. This is likewise true for NBA, NCAA, or any other sports organization. For businesses, including sports, the rush to change America's social mores might prove to be costly rather than profitable. It is, however, the issue of "rights of others" in the taxpayer-funded public forum that comes to the forefront of my mind. A recent Virginia case as well as an ongoing North Carolina case illustrate that one person who "feels psychologically harmed" in being denied certain toilet usage somehow has a greater "right" than another person who equally "feels psychologically harmed" when a person of opposite physical gender uses the toilet.

This is a much different matter than that of certain commercial businesses, entertainers, or sports organizations who leap upon the bandwagon to promote a social cause! Let me state my view with clarity. Persons who may identify themselves as LGBT have the same legal rights and deserve the same respect as do all other persons. But the inverse of that is also true. It is time for our courts and our society to recognize this and act accordingly.

Here is what "push the agenda" people tend to forget. Let's look at the public school issue (though the same would be true for public libraries, parks, or other such taxpayer-funded facilities). One person's demand for "rights" has a negative effect upon another person's pocketbook. Why? Because schools will have to be renovated – at taxpayer expense – to accommodate the demand for unisex toilets necessary if schools wish to respond to the "rights" of the few without sacrificing the similar "rights" of the many. Schools typically are organized into school districts. In this nation there are today an estimated 13,500 public school districts serving about 50 million students in 98,500 schools. Taxpayers provide the funds for these school districts. So when Susie "feels like" she is really Sammy those taxpayers have a right to thoughtfully consider whether, when, and how to retrofit buildings.

Odd as it may seem, our commercial establishments are in a better position to take the lead on the "bathroom" issue. The "Target" approach, however, is counterproductive for it adds fuel to the fire. A more productive measure would be to do what many commercial establishments already have done. Build unisex bathrooms.

But for tax-supported buildings such a change requires both political decisions and funding. This is where respect for the rights of all comes to the fore. School districts, city, county, and state governmental agencies must begin a long-term taxpayer supported campaign to retrofit existing buildings and to design future facilities with unisex bathrooms in mind.

Finally, lest I be branded a hate-mongering homophobic, allow me to share how I have come to respect those who identify themselves as members of the LGBT community. My Bible says that we humans are "created in the image of

God." There are two very key words there. The first is "created." I'll let that stand for the moment for it is a different topic. The second is "image." To be an image of an object is not to be the object itself. Hence we humans lack the totality, the completeness, the perfection of the Creator.

I would argue that each human being lacks our Creator's perfection in unique ways. Just as each human being is composed of the same basic DNA ingredients, yet the DNA menu allows each of us to be identifiable uniquely. So I reason that some of us have a yet-to-be-identified variable which accounts for homosexuality. The rest is human will and the struggle to control that will. For the evidence is clear that both heterosexual and homosexual activity can be seen as socially unacceptable when that activity goes beyond proscribed limits. A heterosexual couple copulating atop a restaurant table would surely go "beyond proscribed limits." So, it is clear that the issue is not what you "are" but what you "do" that makes the difference. And some of us have more difficult choices to make than others.

But we humans tend to dislike restrictions upon our freedoms, and some of us express our freedom one way – including self-restraint – while some do so in another way. Today we seem ever more disinclined to agree on definitions for "proscribed limits."

I say all of this in an attempt to demonstrate to the LGBT community and to all others that I do respect the conditions under which we are struggling. I am attempting to be non-judgmental about those conditions. It is not the conditions of sexual identity I am addressing.

What I am addressing is lack of respect for one another and for one another's rights. For example, a law permitting same gender marriage ought not compel the clergy of any religious institution to perform such a marriage just as the right of free speech does not compel one person to listen to another's free speech.

Hence, the question we all need to be addressing is that of how we can work together to build a multi-faceted society whose foundation is built upon respect for all.

-30-

Trump on Rigged

When Donald Trump says things are "rigged," he is neither whining nor fibbing. Thanks to Associated Press we have a perfect example. Two "journalists" –they are not journalists or they would behave as such – provide evidence to support Trump's claim.

"Trump Insurance Claim Raises Questions" (Star October 25, 2016) raises questions to be sure, but not those the writers intended. Horwitz and Spencer prove to readers, and to Trump, that they are not sufficiently educated to claim the title "journalist." Or, they prove themselves to be "journalists" operating as pimps for the Hillary camp. You be the judge!

The article insinuates that Trump did something wrong by accepting a $17 million insurance payment for storm damage to a Trump property. These two "journalists" interviewed and quoted only two individuals. One a "longtime former butler" for Trump and the other a Palm Beach planning administrator. Are these primary sources for such a story" No!

Do either Horwitz or Spencer display the common knowledge that insurance companies protect themselves from financial skullduggery? That they use claims investigators and adjusters? That they have and use fraud investigators? No!

Did our authors interview any of these insurance professionals? No!

Did our authors identify the particular insurance company for this claim? No!

Did our authors read the policy in question? No!

But they do tell us that the "Associated Press found little evidence of such large scale damage."

Really? When did AP look? The damage in question was eleven years ago! When did AP get into the claims assessment business? Who in AP? Do journalists of today no longer use attribution, or even know what that is?

This article lacks even the most elementary rudiments of journalistic tenets. By accident? By design? Are we beginning to grasp what Trump means when he says "rigged"? This is but one example.

-30-

On Truth? Facts? Today's Journalism

Truth? Facts? Problem is, I don't believe many of us these days want either of those. No, we'd rather go forth with our own opinions without regard to truth or facts. Especially if said truth or facts interfere with what we already believe. And a huge issue here is this: Who can we trust to offer us either truth or facts?

There was a time when I thought I could answer that question. Today is not that time. I no longer know who I can trust to offer truth. And facts? Much the same. But I do know what I can do to begin to remedy the problem. I – and you – can demand better journalism!

Today's writers – I am reluctant even to call many of them journalists – often and blatantly ignore the most basic of journalism tenets. The result is that we readers or viewers are fed neither truth nor fact.

So, what are some of the basics of journalism that are being ignored? And why should we concern ourselves about such? Let me first address the second question. The answer is simple: *If we do not care enough to demand the best of journalism, we'll have to remain content with the worst.* Here, then, are some flaws – intentional or otherwise – in the application of today's "journalism."

First, misrepresenting opinion for fact. Any statement beginning with *good, better,* or *best,* (or any synonym of these) is opinion. Likewise, the word "will." *Will* is future tense, and neither you nor I know factually what "will" happen tomorrow much less ten-minutes from now.

Should, must, and ought are words of advice, hence opinion. Many adjectives - especially those ending with -able, -ible or -less - are opinion words.

Also, keep a keen eye - or ear - for supposition, speculation, and any other form of guesswork. Writing factual information is hard work. So many "journalists" would prefer to be "analysts" or "commentators."

Second, failing to identify sources. This is often called attribution. "A White House spokesperson" is not an adequate source. We readers must distrust whatever follows such a "source." Likewise any other unidentified non-specific source.

Next, qualified sources. If we want information about what happened in Benghazi we ask surviving participants, not Hollywood celebrities. A recent Associated Press article blatantly disregarded standard journalism in a story on a "supposed" insurance fraud. The writers interviewed only two people. Neither was an agent of the insurance agency. Nor did the writers have, or read, the policy in question. So, why did they write the story? Good question.

The point here is not to offer a mini-course in journalism. It is to improve our listening and reading skills so that we might detect whether we are being offered fact or opinion. Today we are confronted with "fake news" to an extent heretofore unimagined. Only when we demand a return to basic, factual, journalism will we have a better chance of being served facts and truth.

--30—

On How dark the heart

Jill Wintersteen has offered us food for thought in her article addressing certain LGBTQ remarks by Del. Dave LaRock. She describes Mr. LaRock in much the same way Jesus describes the Pharisees.

But Wintersteen's food is more a snack than a banquet. Yes, Jesus does model for us compassion, forgiveness, and radical openness. And, yes, this same Jesus would not at all be pleased with "those who think they can openly harass and insult others...."

Yet Jesus offers us much more than gentleness. Alas some of what He has to say will not seem gentle to those who practice homosexuality. Before proceeding, please note the word "practice." This is where so many of us err when addressing topics related to homosexuality. We fail to distinguish between the "being" and the "doing."

Now, I have yet to find any answer to why one person may "be" homosexual and another not. For this reason, I have come to use the word "variant" when thinking on the topic.

Despite being born "in the likeness and image" of God, we humans come to "be" with many variants. Any of us can draw up a list of such variants. Each "variant" poses certain challenges in life. Homosexuality presents seemingly impossible challenges. Can one "be" and yet not "do"?

Let's let that question hang a minute while we return to Jesus. Indeed, not everything He says is gentle: "You brood of vipers!" to the Pharisees. "Get behind me, Satan!" to

Peter. "You belong to your father, the devil...." to the Pharisees. And many more.

But perhaps the most important thing Jesus says with respect to the topic of homosexuality is this: "Do not think that I have come to abolish the Law or the Prophets; I have not come to abolish them but to fulfill them." He added, "... not the smallest letter, not the least stroke of a pen, will by any means disappear from the Law until everything is accomplished."

Now what "Law" do we suppose Jesus is speaking about? Well, that would be the first five books of the Bible, the Torah. One of these is Leviticus within which chapters 18 and 20 make clear what Jesus and His Father think of "practicing" homosexuality. And for those who think Leviticus is only for Levite priests, look again. The Apostle Paul - whom Jesus not so gently recruited - offers the same advice in Romans 1.

So now you know why I spoke of Wintersteen's "snack." That's the way too many of us read the Bible. We should read books and chapters rather than cafeteria-style selected verses.

As for the "being" and not "doing" of homosexuality, that's called abstinence. It's a choice. Difficult. More difficult than being Helen Keller? I can't answer that. But I can tell you this. Jesus abhors homosexual practice the same as He abhors adultery. And He loves all who love Him. Read the rest of the Bible and you'll find that to be true regardless of human "variants."

On Women's Choice

Justine asks:

Was the end result of this editorial, that you are against pro choice?

This may surprise you, but I am absolutely in favor of pro choice. I begin with the recognition that the word "choice" when saying "pro choice" is rendered in the singular and not in the plural. But those who demonstrate and raise their voices on the topic seldom wish to recognize the truth, or reality, of what they are shouting about. Most often those who say "pro choice" are actually speaking about a second choice. That makes it plural, right? They want to choose what to do with the baby which resulted from an earlier choice.

So we're really talking about pro choices, aren't we? And that is what my editorial is about. I'm writing about how we choose to hide the fact, ignoring elemental biology, that once that first choice has been made, the laws of nature will spell out the consequences. We cannot have it both ways. We cannot "get" pregnant and not "be" pregnant. There is, of course, another matter of plurality when we speak of pro choice. The choice women speak of here is not theirs alone. Back to biology 101. Isn't there a male somehow paired with a female? So, yes, I favor pro choice. I favor choosing wisely the first time. If we do so, there'll be no need for that second choice. (See *)

By the way, I revisited that topic we discussed at our most recent gathering around your parents' table. You'll recall we discussed the donation or sale of an ovum. And my view pretty much centers around the same factors I drew upon for this editorial. We humans have developed methods to circumvent the laws of nature. The result is that we are today capable of a choice between artificial and natural. Artificial is the work of man. Natural is the work of God. It may surprise you that our nation's forefathers recognized this distinction more clearly than do we today. Notice. "...the Laws of Nature and of Nature's God...." These words are found within the first paragraph of our Declaration of Independence. Notice the capitalization. More importantly, if you reflect upon it, you'll notice that Thomas Jefferson --along with the other 55 men who signed that document -- acknowledges both the existence of God and of God's creation of the Laws of Nature. (That's why Jefferson used an apostrophe when he wrote "Nature's God.")

So you see, the question of what might reasonably be done with an ovum addresses the same issue: one choice is that of the artificial; the other is that of the natural. And since I agree with Jefferson and all who signed the Declaration of Independence, my choice is to remain with Nature's God.

Finally, just to be politically incorrect, I oppose government support, especially financial support, of groups, agencies, or institutions which engage in abortion (like Planned Parenthood), or which engage in embryonic research. If you are not clear on the differences between embryonic research and stem cell research, we can discuss that another time.

For now, I hope I have answered your question. And I cherish the opportunity for us to have these conversations. I respect you and recognize your intelligence and your good heart. I am certain you will continue to search out the best answers for you as you continue to grow in experience, engaged with a complex world.

(*Back to biology 101)

*Those who promote the women's choice issue are pursuing not "rights" but a political agenda developed to defend abortion, and to compel the federal government to pay –at taxpayer expense) for abortions. For if the issue were truly about "rights" then even the women would have to recognize the rights of two other individuals. The rights of the father, and the rights of the unborn child. But those rights along with the basic facts of Biology 101 are cast aside in the pursuit of self interest.

Let's review some inescapable basics of Biology 101:

- Cell: basic unit of living matter, capable of carrying out all the functions necessary for life.
- Gamete: Sexual reproductive cell (sperm or egg) that unites with another cell to form a new organism.
- Organism: form of life composed of mutually interdependent parts that maintain various vital (living) processes.
- Fertilization: union of one male with one female sex cell (called gametes) from which a new individual (living organism) develops. (Elapsed time: ½ hour to 24-hours).
- DNA: self-duplicating molecule within the nucleus of living cell, agent of self-duplication.
- Chromosome: Threadlike bodies within cell nuclei, carries genetic information including gender.

- Genes: Carriers (upon chromosomes) of genetic information including gender.

These are basic definitions found within any basic biology book, high school or college. Ignoring them does not change the facts.

One cell is life. Two cells are likewise life. The only differences between a fertilized cell and a child at birth are the number of cells and the types of cells. So, again: One cell is life. Two or more cells are likewise life.
Abortion ends a life.
Cannot escape that fact.

The "women's right" movement is a political agenda that chooses to ignore basic science. Like other political movements, the goal is to form a group of like-minded people. Then, from that group, form a bloc of voters. Put many of those blocs together and we have a party appealing to many.

Odd, though. The rainbow coalition of LGBT folks doesn't really care a whit about abortion. Two males or two females are not the ingredients for pregnancy. Hence, little interest in the abortion issue. So that group becomes a separate voting bloc. And on it goes.

Finally, please do not also ignore the word "information" in several of those definitions above. You are capable, if you choose to do so, of grasping the nature of "information."

About Those 56 men

If today we were to find fifty-six men who would publicly proclaim such statements as these, the likelihood is that each and every one of these men would be cast as pariahs of society. They would be shunned. They would be ridiculed. They'd likely receive a summons, be hauled into court, and be indicted for engaging in a "hate crime." Punitive actions against such men would be justified, many would agree, even if all fifty-six of them were successful businessmen, members of respected community organizations, or elected local government officials from mayor to governor.

What sort of statement or proclamation might spawn such public chastisement? Well, here are four candidate statements:

> There is a deity who has established the laws of nature, and this deity is God.
>
> There is a Creator who has created all men.
>
> There is a Supreme Judge of the world to whom all may appeal in times of peril.
>
> There is a Divine Provider of protection upon whom all can rely.

Many citizens of today hold such speech to be medieval utterances of the feeble minded. Do we not consider this type of speech to be unsuitable in the public forum? Controversial commentary of this type ought to be restricted to the confines of churches! And surely, candidates for public office ought never be elected after making statements like these.

And yet fifty-six men did publicly make these very proclamations! They boldly put their signatures to the statements and risked their very lives in doing so! Surely they must have realized that the courts have enacted prohibitions against promoting religious beliefs in public surroundings. Where did these Bible-thumpers come from?

Well, that part we can answer. They came from Delaware, New Jersey, Connecticut, Pennsylvania, and New York. Some were from New Hampshire, others from Georgia, North and South Carolina, and Rhode Island. A few were from Virginia and Maryland. Five were from Massachusetts.

They had ordinary names like William, John, and Samuel. Some were George, a few were Thomas. One or two had rather unique names. Not so common was a fellow called Button. Another was named Caesar. Altogether, the fifty-six men had the look of commonplace Americans.

But what they proclaimed – well, as noted, it was controversial at the very least. And probably criminal. Today.

After all, they did claim that there is God. Not just "a" God. God. Creator. Divine. And according to all fifty-six of these men, God created all men!

Isn't it politically incorrect, unacceptable, to speak this way? In America? The land of the tolerant? It would seem so. Today. But these were fifty-six men who "hold these truths to be self-evident."

Surely, by now, most of you have recognized the source of what these men proclaimed. You have also probably guessed the date. Sure, July, 1776.

So, were these men “wackos” or delirious ne’er-do-wells? Not at all. They were the authors and signatories of our Nation’s Declaration of Independence!

So what has changed in our country?

-30-

House of lies

When we build a house of lies, we ought to expect calamity. After all, lying is dishonest. To be avoided at all costs, right? So we don't lie. Rather, when we are uncomfortable with truth, we find ways to dance around it. We play the game of "What we call it" to avoid owning up to "What it is." And we play this game, and we allow our government to play this game, on the most serious of issues. Things like life, death, and abortion.

Tragically, the game goes on virtually unnoticed until something macabre rips at our conscience. Something like selling a baby's liver. That's impossible to "not notice."
But how did we slide into such degradation? We began many years ago when we played the game of "What we call it." Not comfortable with the word "baby" when discussing certain issues, we resorted to other terms. "Fetus" and "embryo" began to appear in the newspapers. After all, who wants to say "baby" when discussing abortion?

We slid to where we are today when we began to ignore, and to willfully redefine, how human life begins. Understanding the truth is not actually all that complicated. Reduced to the basics, the formula is this: sperm + ovum = human cell. We call this process fertilization. And once fertilization takes place what follows is a steady increase in numbers of cells and types of cells.

I refreshed my memory a day or two ago, and came up with this summary:
A fertilized human cell begins to divide repeatedly. The rest of the process is numbers and types. As cells divide the

number of cells increases. Then cells begin to differentiate, different types of cells result. These different types will become different organs. So, at the instant of fertilization (sperm + egg = cell), the number and types of cells begin to increase. The simple term for this process is growth.

Those two key words "process" and "growth" are central to understanding the truth about human life. Life itself is a process. Beginning, maturation, end. That's the process in the simplest of terms.

Now consider "growth." That which grows has life. True for humans, true for animals, true for plants. Stated another way, if it's growing it's alive. If it's alive, it has life. Now returning to that fertilized human cell, consider this. Given roughly 270 days, the number and types of human cells will have grown to the point at which life within the womb is ready to commence to life outside the womb. So, the only differences between that first fertilized cell and the human being which emerges at birth are time and growth.

Now returning to the lies. Until recently, some 55 million abortions in our nation have been shrouded with the lies which began with the "What we call it" game. We have allowed our consciences to be soothed by hiding behind terms like fetus, embryo, and abortion. Only those who make the effort to consult a dictionary will come to notice the truth. A fetus is a human life. An embryo is a human life. An abortion is the termination of a human life. It's that simple. The rest is choice.

Oh, and one more lie, this one best revealed with a question. How is an organization called Planned Parenthood related to the word "parenthood"?

-30-

A Silver Lining?

Behind every cloud a silver lining? With no wish to ignore the thousands of personal tragedies, the deaths, or the families ripped asunder by Harvey and Irma, there is another aspect to consider as recovery begins. Our focus is called to costs. Small wonder when we see Government deployment of first responders followed by emergency care and fiscal relief. We rightly are concerned about cost. What taxpayer wouldn't be? But it's easy to overlook the secondary fiscal impact.

Those thousands of utility linemen streaming into Florida are already at work. And "at work" is the key phrase. Some may be volunteers, but most are employed. They are earning wages. Those wages are taxed. Taxes that ultimately return to the same Federal and State governments now disbursing financial aid to victims.

Now look to the hundreds of thousands of soggy, moldy mattresses being dragged to curbsides from Texas to Florida. What were yesterday's king, queen, and twin-sized bedding are today's trash. Same story for all upholstered furniture! Sofas, chairs, footstools. Maybe some wooden or metal items will be salvageable. But tons upon tons of yesterday's stuffed-chairs are now piling up for disposal.

Extremely bad news for home owners and renters alike. But. For the furniture manufacturing industry, it's time to go into production mode! Overtime for employees. New hires for increased staffing.

Enter the packing, shipping, and delivery industry. Everything is needed now! Mattresses, sofas, carpet, and construction material of all kinds. Untold tons of drywall must be installed along the entire coast of Texas and all of Florida! Refrigerators, freezers. Mountains of rotted foodstuffs. So much to replace!

More bad news for victims. Cars, trucks, RV's, boats. The family van. Not to mention auto dealers both "new" and "used." Thousands upon thousands of vehicles submerged by salty, contaminated water. Most of these cannot be repaired.

Enter the automobile industry. Ramp up production! Now. Hire, now! More production. More wages. More shipping for components. More delivery! And all of this economic boost of activity will result in increased tax revenue at every level from State to Federal.

Now, I'm no economist! But surely there are "formulas" for this sort of thing. This secondary economic tax-revenue-producing rebound. Skilled workers, perhaps many who have been under-employed in recent years, are streaming into Texas and Florida. Roads, bridges, water pipes, sewage-disposal. So much to repair!

My challenge? I would welcome someone more qualified than I to really dig deep into this aspect of the stories of Harvey and Irma. It's not about political advantage (there'll be more than enough candidate back-slapping). It's about the American economy. The silver lining behind those dark clouds that brought us all this mess.

P.S. Will someone please ask our elected officials to shed some daylight on the increased tax revenues they might otherwise hide from our view?

-30-

On the "Why" of Writing

It's a reasonable question, I suppose. "Why all this effort on W R I T I N G !" It deserves a reasonable response. Here, from the perspective of one who spent 24 years in uniform, are some of the types of writing we use in the military (and a connection to the business world will not be difficult to notice):

REQUESTS FOR FUNDING or STAFFING:
From an infantry platoon to a wing commander, from pencil-jock to a division four-star, we are all competing for three things: funding, staffing, and equipment. And we all claim what "we" need is "essential" for the mission. We need more ammunition, more aircraft, more people. So, what do we do? We write requests (staff papers). The frog in the muck writes what he wants the eagle in the sky to sign! That's important to remember. What we write is for someone else's signature! Does the colonel (who would very much like to become a general) really want to sign a document that makes him look like a buffoon?

PERFORMANCE EVALUATIONS:
Every person at every level of the operation is evaluated. These written documents become part of the "file" which finds itself upon a desktop somewhere up the chain. Promotion boards! 'Nuf said.

TRAINING DOCUMENTS:
The military life is a life of training and preparation. So we write everything from a list of steps to take, from a "tech" order, from a policy booklet, all the way to entire books and

manuals. Then we improve these documents because some fool botched an assignment. So we revise. And the sun rises. And we revise. Until, "Oh, hell, let's scrap the whole book and come up with a new one." Hmmmm.

EQUIPMENT or OPERATIONAL EVALUATIONS:
We evaluate equipment. Why? Usually because the boss wants to buy something new. (Mission essential, of course!) So we do comparison shopping. Shall it be Apple or Microsoft? A Colt "45" or a Beretta M9-A1? We evaluate operations. What went well? What didn't? Which manual do we need to revise before the next operation?

AFTER-ACTION REPORTS:
We go "TDY" (that's a funded business trip for you civilians). The word "funded" is key here. We traveled somewhere (or we propose to do so) with someone else's money. (Oh, how we wish all "guvvi-ment" folks would remember "whose" money we are using.) We must justify the travel (and hope to fund a future trip). So we write after action reports. Now and then someone reads these things.

JUSTIFICATIONS FOR COMMITMENT of ASSETS:
We get requests from all sorts of agencies, both "civil" and military. Folks want a platoon for a parade here (oh, hell, why not a battalion?), or an F-16 for a fly-by there. Or a flag detail for the parent-teacher association at your kid's school. A formation fly-by at the Indianapolis 500? Or, perhaps the "Super Bowl?" All of this. And more. And guess what. The letter you - the frog in the muck - write will be signed by your boss, endorsed by his boss, sent to higher headquarters by a one-star so a four-star can sign and approve what once was a two-paragraph note but now has

become a six-inch thick operational order to be approved by the USAF Chief of Staff! And some captain at a desk outside the general's office will carefully check that everyone up and down the chain of command has crossed all the tees and dotted all the eyes! (Go ahead. Try to write the letters "t" and "i" in the plural and possessive while not confusing the plural for an apostrophe!) 'Nuf said.

LETTERS TO PARENTS:
Do you really want to write a letter to Private Ryan's mom and have it look like a fourth-grader's crayon poster?

ACCIDENT INVESTIGATION REPORTS:
Stuff happens. And when it does, people write about it. Accident investigation reports find their way all way to Washington and back. What REALLY happened? Why? Who's to blame? How to fix? And, of greatest importance, who is going to re-write the manual so that this never again happens? An F-106 fell out of the sky and burrowed itself into a Montana wheat field. The pilot survived. I had the interesting assignment, once, of compiling, writing, editing, and revising the entire report. I was a "second lieutenant." The accident investigation board was a dozen colonels, lieutenant colonels, majors, and civilian technicians. I learned a lot! Not the least of which was that the pilot was not at fault. (That's important, especially if you happen to be the pilot of that 2.75-million-dollar jet airplane.) At fault was a flange. Damn thing split. Fuel leaked. Fire broke out. And the scientist-tech? He was able to prove that the flange had burned at above 30,000 feet before it implanted itself into the wheat field. Go figure! Look what science can do. But I got to take that information and write a report

that cleared the pilot. He had followed the manual. As written. And that manual has been revised. Hmmm.

INTELLIGENCE & WEATHER BRIEFINGS:
Where is the enemy? What has he got? Will the weather allow us to clobber him? Dozens upon dozens of guys (and gals) are writing briefings - right now - to answer questions like these before a commander somewhere commits his people to a task. More writing. Go figure.

WRITING AND THINKING
And note this: Writing is a process which forces us to think! This may be one of the greatest benefits to writing. While we are pulling together information and data, we find ourselves isolating "the parts" and examining how "things" might "work" best. And what often happens is this: we discover flaws. We sense something is missing. We realize that when someone else reads our work, that someone might ..... Go ahead. Fill the blank. You get the idea.

(I wrote this at the request of a fellow teacher who sought to motivate students who fail to see the need for learning to write.)

I muse

I chanced to walk in a moment too late and so I asked my wife for the title of the film she had tuned in. She didn't remember but said, "It looks interesting." I could easily forgive her short-term memory lapse for both she and I are septuagenarians. You probably guessed as much when I wrote "film" to describe a digitally delivered video.

Within moments I was enmeshed in the story. I had read the novel in 1969. I knew the characters: Spangler, Grogan, Homer, Ulysses, Marcus, Bess. Long-term memory kicks in with greater acuity now that I'm on the far side of seven decades. I even knew the setting: Ithaca, the small if imaginary town with its "Postal Telegraph" office.
A deluge of memories. I was in my twenties as I read the story. In Omaha. A student at the University of Nebraska. A town not unlike that of the 14-year-old telegram delivery boy hired by Spangler. I could identify with Mr. Grogan for I had been doing for the military what he was doing for Spangler's Postal Telegraph office.

It was a momentous time in my life. War. Travel. Death. Families anxiously awaiting word of the fate of soldiers dispatched to far-away places. Not hard to identify with the story, now a film on a 50-inch screen in my living room.
But what was the title? Who was the author? My wife didn't remember the title after five minutes. And I have found such lapses in memory to be highly contagious. I groped for that title right to the gut-wrenching end of the film. So I did what any self-respecting senior citizen would do. I "googled" it. Only to find that the Netflix version is called *Ithaca* and stars Meg Ryan and Tom Hanks. I knew

the 1943 novel as *The Human Comedy* when I read it in 1969.

Now I had "googled" to recover details buried under five of my life's seven decades. Then I began to muse. And the word "if" permeated my musing. I wondered "if" today's youth still read William Saroyan's *The Human Comedy*? Do students know that Saroyan's parents were Armenian immigrants? Do they know why the family emigrated? Can they find Armenia on a world map?

If they have read *The Human Comedy*, do they know which war is central to the story? Was it the war featured in Remarque's *All Quiet on the Western Front*? Or, was it the war known for The Battle of Dunkirk, the Holocaust, and D-Day? And if today's students know of author William Saroyan, do they know why critics called him a "pacifist"? Was "pacifist" in 1943 a patriotic appellation?

Such were my musings as I reflected upon Saroyan's novel, now a film. As for the state of literary education of today's youth, I'll have to text my two granddaughters in California. They live where Saroyan lived. In Fresno. Perhaps they've seen the theater at 730 M Street.

-30-

On global warming

Some of us don't seem to care much about facts these days. Especially abhorrent are facts which disagree with pronouncements made by activists who would prefer for us to believe their views without regard to facts. Or at least without regard to certain facts.

Case in point. Global warming and "ocean temperatures spike" (Star, January 19, 2016). Now I would not presume to argue against global warming. Nor would I consider myself sufficiently erudite to dispute the notion that global warming might result in ocean warming. But I do wish that "scientists" who publish their findings in journals would exhibit a wider range of their academic credentials. I mean, didn't Geology 101 precede a post-graduate scholarly study in the journal Nature Climate Change?

Global warming band-wagoneers from one end of this planet to the other seem to have slept through the first chapter of Geology 101. That's the chapter explaining that our planet has experienced at least five major and several minor periods of "ice ages." Now here's a fact these "scientists" seem to have ignored. Each of those "ice ages" was followed by global warming. How do we know this? Well, for starters, the ice melted.

Of greatest interest to us – the modern day descendants of homo east-coastus-Americus – is the most recent of these many ice ages. You see, that "ice age" of the late Pleistocene epoch is the one whose glaciers, according to New York Nature.net "literally created Long Island, and carved out the landscape we know today as the New York

City region. Moraines, lakes and ponds, kettle holes, peat bogs, melt water streams and valleys – all are relics of glacial topography."

So it seems some scientists use "ice age" information one way, some another. If your business is constructing One World Trade Center, you most assuredly want to know the difference between bedrock and a glacial moraine. But many "scientists" whose favorite topic is global warming seem eager to ignore the lessons of ice ages.

It takes little more than an introduction to Logic 101 for most of us to recognize that for every ice age there has followed a period of global warming. (Please check a geological time scale.) Moreover, climate change is influenced – and has been so for eons – by many factors. Solar energy output varies; both the sun and our planet earth are constantly in motion. Everything out there where "*the heavens declare the glory of God*" is moving. Earth spins (rotates) and races around its orbital path. And so does the Sun whose orbit takes it on a journey through our galaxy. Small wonder, then, that a wobble here and a solar eruption there might result in a pile of ice once and clouds of steam the next time.

So, please. Let us recognize that when we are faced with political posturing and perambulation, we are better off to rely upon facts – even the inconvenient ones – than to beguile ourselves with half-baked writings of "scientists" who slept through Geology 101.

How dare you dishonor

How dare you dishonor the victims, the still-grieving families, and the sacrifices of American military with manipulative journalistic innuendo? (Joseph Lelyveld, Smithsonian, September, 2011, What 9/11 Wrought).

You tell readers, "There was no hard evidence linking at least one-fifth - and possibly more—of the Guantanamo detainees to terrorist movements."

Why did you choose to emphasize the 20% and ignore the 80%? Your statement could as easily have read, "There was hard evidence linking at least eighty-percent of the Guantanamo detainees to terrorist movements."

Did you wish to deemphasize the fact that in a time of great stress and uncertainty and with minimum time for preparation we Americans deployed our military farther than 7,000 miles, rounded up terrorists in hostile lands, and got it right 80% of the time?

No need to answer, Joseph. It's a rhetorical question. You add degradation to dishonor with your oft-repeated "supposed terrorists" and with your stated concerns over "humiliation, physical stress" and later with your misgivings over "conclusions Afghans and Iraqis will draw ... after years of living with the possibility of sudden death."

Why, Joseph, do you fail to see that we prefer the war against terrorists to be on their soil, not ours? Mr. Lelyveld, we want those countries, and others harboring terrorists, to conclude that if they breed and support terrorists who attack

Americans, they must live with the possibility of sudden death. As for me, I am proud of our country's "Don't tread on me" patriotism!

-30-

On Thinking

God gave us intellect. This attribute, intellect, is one of the ways in which we are created in the image of God. Intellect is a tool. He expects us to use it. Consider the parable of the talents (Matt 25: 15, 16). The idea is to use our intellect, not bury it in the ground.

Thinking is how we use intellect. We were born with intellect. Thus, we were born with the capacity to think. This attribute is one of the ways in which we differ from toads. Now don't get me wrong here. I'm not a card-carrying member of the anti-toad association. But until I visit the Toad Library of Congress, tour the facility, read a few toad-authored books, and surf their web page, I'll stick with my assessment that toads lack a key ingredient you and I have and, as noted, are expected to use.

Alas, most of us confuse thinking with day-dreaming. I'll be the first to admit that day-dreaming might eventually lead to more structured thinking. But the two are not the same. Actually, thinking is what ought to follow day-dreaming. What I'm calling day-dreaming, some call creative thinking. Both have their place. We allow a stream of ideas and images flow as we "kick back." In time, if kicking back doesn't result in nodding off, one or more of these fleeting thoughts might lead us to the "aha" moment. If we reach that aha moment and do nothing more, the idea remains just that, a wispy notion, an aquarium without water. To transform the aha moment into something more functional requires ... well, action. Thinking.

So let's examine five critical verbs which go into the act of thinking.

- connect
- compare
- manipulate
- combine
- re-form

We connect when we associate one bit of information or one idea with another. Often this seems to happen by accident. Yet if we actively seek out a "connection" we find ourselves asking mental questions. For example, in church we hear, "*Then repay to Caesar what belongs to Caesar and to God what belongs to God*" (Luke 20:25). We then ask ourselves, "Why Caesar? What has Rome to do with Jesus? Why would Jews pay taxes to Rome?" Soon, we make connections between Luke's Gospel and secular history. We might then connect the paying of taxes to Caesar to the paying of today's taxes to federal, state, and local governments. Further, we might connect that thought with another by asking ourselves what other civic responsibilities might be included under the umbrella idea of "*rendering to Caesar.*" Voting? Keeping abreast of issues? Being knowledgeable about candidates, and office holders? You get the point.

We compare when we examine one idea and mentally seek similarities and differences between that idea and another. On a mundane level, we often compare when shopping as we consider price, quantity or volume, or we assess features and quality of similar items. When we compare we are seeking similarities. For example, Job and Jonah seem similar in at least one respect. Both expressed disappointment in God. But comparing quickly brings to the table its cousin, contrasting. While to compare is to focus chiefly on similarities, to contrast is to examine differences. Both are essential ingredients of the thinking process. Differences between Job and Jonah soon become quite apparent. One of them seems to be a victim. The other rather brazenly disobeys God. If you're not sure which is which, that's okay. This is where curiosity enters the picture. Curiosity and thinking often result in discovering a need to reacquaint oneself with facts. Thinkers, being mentally active, will reach for the book, in this case the Bible, for a quick refresher.

We manipulate when we literally take a hands-on approach to examining something. The Latin *manus* leads to English *manual*, as in manual labor. To manipulate an idea, we do something with it. Play with it (mentally), play with the words, rearrange them. Look for words within words. Imagine what must have come immediately before an action and what might logically follow it. When viewing television video or news photos, always ask yourself what is not "on camera." What was going on to the left, to the right, and behind that cameraman? Ask, "What's wrong with (or missing from) this picture?" Ask why the reporter included this or avoided that in a news account. Ask yourself, "Who gains and who loses in this proposal or action?" Do the math! Always immediately think of the opposite number. If reporters tell us 40% favor proposition A, immediately remind yourself about the 60% who do not favor it! If the report tells us fifty-thousand gathered to demonstrate at an anti-name-your-issue rally, compare that figure, that fifty-thousand, with the city's population. After all, fifty-thousand is fewer than the number of spectators attending one NFL football game. A different mental picture is sure to emerge.

Besides, half of those demonstrators probably came from out-of-town if not from some other country. And another 10% may have simply noticed the crowd and edged up to take a closer look. Always question the "facts."

Focus on the difference between fact and opinion (watch for any synonym of *good-better-best,* and for *should* or *will).* Also, convert numbers until you find something recognizable. Ruth, we learn in the Bible, gleaned "*about an ephah*" of barley. An ephah is clearly a unit of measurement. After you refresh your memory on such things as bushels and pecks, you'll find, as I did, that what Ruth gleaned (Ruth 3:17) amounted to about five one-gallon milk jugs filled with grain! I don't know about you, but my mind immediately starts to wonder how many loaves of bread Ruth and Naomi might bake with that much grain.

Finally, manipulate by translating from one language to another as you read or listen. Or, trace the origin of a word, think of related words, find words within words. Try recasting a statement in reverse. Literally, turn it inside-out. Identify what it is not.

We combine when we mix or blend one idea or concept with another. Actually, this could be thought of as a subset of manipulate. Some creative television commercials come to mind here. A truck filled with smooth milk chocolate collides with another carrying a ton of peanut butter. Presto! We've got a new candy bar. Two angels in heaven. One has cream cheese, the other strawberries. They stumble, and, you guessed it. Something new to spread on your toasted bagel.

We re-form when we blend two or more ideas and come up with something new, original, or at least distinctively different. Blend a car with a boat. Now we've got an amphibious vehicle. Military folks use them, but so do civilians. Tourists in Santa Barbara, California, can ride the "Land Shark," a Hydra Terra amphibious vehicle manufactured in New York State. Such vehicles can go from highway to waterway without stopping. Re-forming two vehicles into one is probably easier than what our Lord asked us to re-form. Jesus taught us to re-form our thinking when He said, "*You have heard that it was said, 'You shall love your neighbor and hate your enemy.' But I say to you, love your enemies, and pray for those who persecute you, that you may be children of your heavenly Father*" (Matthew 5:43-45). Hmmm. That does require some thinking.

Think about thinking. And when you do engage in thinking, think about *how* you are thinking. You might be on your way to a better understanding of, well, even God! After all, He wants us to discover Him. He gave us intellect. And like the parable of the ten gold coins (Luke 19:11), God expects us to use this gift and not say, "I kept it stored away in a handkerchief" as did one servant. Think. Then think about thinking. Exercise that gift. Make it grow!

Rapping a Senator's Knuckles

Dear Senator Sessions (and others crowing over his Sotomayor preliminary statement):

I address the Senator:

> *If we wish to achieve success in opposing a candidate, a proposal, or a piece of legislation, we must avoid the nebulous. We must return to "Debate 101" and back our assertions with concrete support. Otherwise we fail our cause by being indistinguishable from our opponents.*

Sessions speaks of judicial philosophy. I counter:

Of interest is that "*justice*" is rendered here as an adjective. It specifies a particular type of philosophy. The author recognizes that Republicans and Democrats accept the concept of a judicial philosophy even if they disagree on the particulars of such. Of greater interest here is the word being modified. Most scholars, whether or not they are legislators, would agree that *philosophy* (*Gr. loving + wisdom*) refers to a systematic examination of concepts of *truth, existence, reality, causality*, and *freedom*. The word also is a noun expressing a set of *beliefs* or *aims*. In this capacity philosophy joins its fellow synonyms *precepts, principles, attitudes, values, and beliefs*. It is instructive here to recognize that each of these (italicized words) is an abstract noun. As such, these words are not material, objective, concrete, or measurable in nature. Perhaps that is why politicians prefer *principles* over pineapples!

Sessions speaks of impartial application of law. I counter:

To be neutral, objective, and open-minded does not restrict a judge from applying knowledge gained by virtue of one's environment. What child does not know, "It takes one to know one"? Who knows a female better than another female? Who knows a Latina better than ...... okay, you get the point. Knowledge is the product of many things. One's environment is one of those many things. Thus, the "judicial" issue is not "Do you have a *Weltanschauung*"? Rather it is, "How do you, judge, apply the law to this case?"

Sessions speaks of applying the law to the facts. I counter.

The law is not applied to facts. It is applied to people, or more specifically, to the actions (or the inactions) of people.

Sessions states: (A judge must) impartially apply the law to the facts without regard to personal views. This is the compassionate system, because it's the fair system.

I counter: Impartially (noted above), compassionate, fair – three more abstract terms, in this case adverb and adjectives. Please note these synonyms for compassionate: sympathetic, empathetic, caring, concerned, and feeling. Also note the opposite of compassionate: unfeeling. Would not Sotomayor thank you for acknowledging the need for a "compassionate system"?

Sessions states: That oath reads, "I do solemnly swear that I will administer justice without respect to persons, and to equal right to the rich and the poor, and that I will faithfully and impartially discharge and perform all the duties incumbent upon me under the Constitution and laws of the United States, so help me God."

I counter: One or more words are missing from this oath. Someone please give the senator a corrected copy of the oath.

Sessions states: ...impartial and wise judge guides us to truth:

I counter: A wise judge? Wisdom's synonyms are: understanding, knowledge, insight, and perception among others. And what is the source of understanding if not the application of knowledge beyond the prima facie? Sotomayor smiles once again.

Sessions states: ...who believes it is acceptable for a judge to allow their personal background, gender, prejudices or sympathies to sway their decision:

I counter: The grammar here is as weak as the argument. The antecedent to "their" cannot be "a judge." The argument is weakened by your previous reference to a wise judge.

No, I, the author of this critique am not a Democrat. Nor am I a Liberal. (I acknowledge that *liberal* is another of those abstract notions. Here I am referring to political affiliation.) Rather, I am a Republican from the Mid-west. And here, in conclusion, is my point: **If we wish to achieve success in opposing a candidate, a proposal, or a piece of legislation, we must avoid the nebulous. We must return to "Debate 101" and back our assertions with concrete**

support. Otherwise we fail our cause by being indistinguishable from our opponents.

If we oppose the appointment of a judge, cite actual cases and decisions (are these not a matter of public record?). Demonstrate with a verifiable "track record" why we oppose what we oppose!

And, for the record, please note this "reality check." Do the math. Sotomayor's appointment will be a reflection of the numerical realities of the Senate. And these numbers were known prior to the hearings. But Senators do enjoy the cameras, and that, fellow Americans, is what the hearings are about!

-30-

GOD IS LOVE IS GOD

God is.
And because God is, I am, we are.
God created all, including me, including you.
But why?
One word.
Love.
Again, but why?
One word.
Reciprocity.
Love is not complete, cannot be complete, until received and then returned.
Give, receive, return.
Without reciprocity, love withers, love dies.
One word.
Choice.
God freely gives love. We freely choose to receive His love.
Or not.
We freely choose to return love.
Or not.
Had He not created us,
God's love would remain incomplete.
We complete God's gift of love.
When we choose.
Receive. Return. Reciprocate.

....

"God is" in 100 words.

Based on: *God is love; and he that dwells in love dwells in God, and God in him.* (1 JOHN 4:16)

On Jesus and Homosexuality

I Differ with Professor
OPEN Forum June 23

May I respectfully differ with one who differs with me?

Though I lack your professor of religion credentials, Mr. Copenhaver, I do detect that you demonstrate a shortcoming common to many who read the Bible. We need to read with the Paul Harvey "rest of the story" approach. When we do so, we can avoid some of the pitfalls we create with omission. Allow me to refresh our readers' minds by quoting from what I actually wrote May 10, 2017:

But perhaps the most important thing Jesus says with respect to the topic of homosexuality is this: "Do not think that I have come to abolish the Law or the Prophets; I have not come to abolish them but to fulfill them." He added, "... not the smallest letter, not the least stroke of a pen, will by any means disappear from the Law until everything is accomplished."
Now what "Law" do we suppose Jesus is speaking about? Well, that would be the first five books of the Bible, the Torah. One of these is Leviticus within which chapters 18 and 20 make clear what Jesus and His Father think of "practicing" homosexuality. And for those who think Leviticus is only for Levite priests, look again. The Apostle Paul – whom Jesus not so gently recruited – offers the same advice in Romans 1.

So that I might better grasp what God offers us from Genesis to Revelation, I prefer to read the whole Bible, not solely the parts that conform to my fondest desires for humanity. You have told our readers that Jesus "never speaks about" homosexual practice. But you err! He does so in Matthew 5 which I quoted above. True, Jesus does not utter the words "homosexual, homosexuality, or orientation." But He does clearly tell us that He neither abolishes nor changes the Law. And you as a Bible scholar surely know the "Law" he speaks of. And you know where to find this verse:

"*'Do not have sexual relations with a man as one does with a woman; that is detestable.*"

So, yes, Jesus does speak "of" homosexuality. This is not manipulation of the Bible, Professor. And, yes, those texts are relevant today, contrary to your statement otherwise. Do you believe Jesus errs when he says *"... not the smallest letter, not the least stroke of a pen, will by any means disappear from the Law until everything is accomplished"*? Do you believe everything has been accomplished?

Finally, my article did not say Jesus abhors the homosexual person, or, for that matter, the adulterous person. You and I both know what He does abhor. Actions which preclude our eternal union with Him. He wants us. He wants us to want Him. We must all want Him enough to sacrifice that which He abhors. For homosexuals that sacrifice is an act of love He will not forget.

For the record, I am Frank Tilton, not Tipton. Please remember that when you submit transcripts.

On Toothbrushes and Phones

A stranger walks directly into my home, picks up my toothbrush and begins to brush his teeth. "No!" I protest. "This is not okay!"

Not only is it not okay, it's disgusting. Besides. I paid for that toothbrush, not to mention the toothpaste!

This same scenario plays out every day. A dozen times a day. With my telephone. Why is it that every Tom, Sally, and Harry thinks it's perfectly okay to use my telephone – whether cell or landline – to conduct their business?

I bought the phone. I pay the monthly service fee. But others waltz right in and use my phone. They want me to buy something. They seek a donation. Or, more sinister, they want to convince me there is something wrong with my computer which only they can fix!

No! This is not okay! It's my phone. I get to decide how to use it. I will do everything in my power to block your call. Failing that, I will cut you off in mid-sentence without so much as an apology! I will exercise my right to use my phone my way.

And, by the way. I promise not to burst into your home and use your toothbrush! Fair enough?

On Evil and Free Will

To Jordan Peterson

Were it not for your light-hearted tongue-partially-in-cheek Curriculum Vitae (final page of "12 Rules"), I probably would not have made bold to write you. But I sensed there and elsewhere within your book a humble honesty rarely found within such pages of erudite discourse. So I'll offer a stab at addressing your puzzlement (pg 46) over the meaning of the "creature in the garden." Like you, I'll save my Curriculum Vitae for the end. But up front I'll fess up, I lack your (well deserved) credentials. I am not priest, pastor, or professor. I am but a septuagenarian who yet retains curiosity.

There are two key words I find useful in explaining the creature in the garden. The first is love. The second is free will. (Okay, that's three words. Bear with me.) Not long ago I found myself writing an essay to my 21-year-old grandson. On Love. Mostly I think my thoughts were original, but in truth more like today's humus derived from yesterday's granite mountain peaks.

Let's begin with free will. I find it truly this simple. In the absence of evil, there exists no choice for good. Genesis does not say, "Let there be evil," but it is evident the Author of Life created, or at least, permitted, the presence of evil. I suppose it matters little whether "evil" is depicted as a serpent, but its presence is essential. It is the sine qua non of good and of choice.

Closely related is the matter of love. Here is what I explained to my grandson:

Love by its very nature is a relationship of reciprocity. Love is not complete, cannot be complete, until received and then returned. Without reciprocity, love withers, love dies. The reciprocity of love is like an oval. The giving is complete only with the receiving. The receiving responds with giving in return. The original giver becomes the recipient who again becomes the giver. God freely gives love. We freely choose to receive His love. Or not. We freely choose to return His love. Or not. Had He not created us, God's own love would remain incomplete! We humans complete God's gift of love. We do so when we choose to receive, to return, to reciprocate. Oddly enough, even God with all His power cannot complete the cycle of love without human response. Love, then, is both reciprocal and symbiotic.

So, yes, there is cause for puzzlement. After all, who would believe that God couldn't do it alone! All the more reason to treat ourselves as if we are someone responsible for helping God. What a beautiful chapter!

On Wisdom and Careful Reading

To Jordan Peterson-2

[With reference to "12 Rules" Rule 7, page 162]

I think I understand why you did what you did. But I am as close to certain as I can be that few of your readers will follow your reasoning.

You begin page 162 with satire, and, yes, most of your serious readers will perceive that. They will know your intent is not to convince people that they should "lie, cheat, steal deceive, manipulate" and "live for the moment."

But even I, a careful reader, was taken aback by what followed. You quote portions of the Bible's *Book of Wisdom*, and you do so incorrectly, or at least incompletely. And yes, I know you are using The Revised Standard Version. But few of your Protestant readers are likely to be familiar with that version, and many (less well-rounded) Protestants – those who even recognize the Book of Wisdom – will shudder with distrust when they realize (if they realize) that they are reading Apocrypha.

So, you've lost some readers right there. That's okay. Your book. Your choice.

But what is not so okay is how you have edited the selection identified as Wisdom 2: I-II. You have omitted the first eight words of verse 1. And, yes, I perceive your point. But I fear many will not. In my Bible (NAB) – I would use RSV if I had one – those first words are: "*they who said among themselves, thinking not aright:*"

Alas, without that *thinking not aright*, inattentive readers will likely read the rest of the selection and come to the conclusion that, "Gosh, I didn't know that Bible said that!"

Of course, you and I and hopefully more than a handful of your readers will see the satire corresponding to what you wrote at the top of page 162.

But the "*Book of Wisdom*" is not only viewed by many as Apocrypha, and therefore not likely to be available for inspection, it is also one of those books which ancient editors have divided into chapters and verses differently from what modern readers might expect. That is why Chapter 2 begins with an uncapitalized word (*they*) which, in this case, is the continuation of a sentence begun in Chapter 1. The result of this is that for complete understanding of Chapter 2's opening verse, one must read verse 16 of Chapter 1.

That is why I opined above that you had incorrectly or incompletely quoted the piece.

My concern, then, remains. Thank you for bearing with me. Should you in future produce a second edition, you might consider an artful revision here.

On Being Traumatized by the Bible

One cannot reasonably, logically, or legally exercise one's freedom of speech or religion while simultaneously denying that same right to another!

We live in a complex society. There is need at all times to be respectful of the rights of all. But not all in our Nation see respect for rights as a two-way street. Case in point. An Air Force Base in Wyoming has an ongoing case pitting some opposed to the Bible against others favoring it. These are uniformed military members, each of whom having sworn by oath to support and defend the Constitution of this Nation. That prompted me to write to the Secretary of the Air Force:

Madam Secretary, with due respect to your office, your career, and your education, may I suggest that you revisit fundamental realities of the nature of "rights" emanating from our Constitution and its source documents?

At the core of many of today's conflicts over "rights" is this fact: One person's right – of freedom of speech or religion, for example -- does not obviate that same right from another. Correspondingly, one's exercise of free speech does not obligate another person to listen.

That said, as background, I am referring to an incident at Warren Air Force Base wherein a base commander has been approached by members of the unit who apparently feel "disturbed" (one report said "traumatized") by the presence of a Bible upon a table.

At the risk of trivializing that which is utterly serious, may I point out that a Bible is like a radio. The fact that it rests upon a table does not obligate anyone to switch it on.

Additionally, in all of recorded human history there is not a single account of a Bible having attacked or terrorized a human being.

Madam Secretary, you and I both know that seeing a Bible upon a table in no way obligates a person to read it. We also know the source of this conflict. That source is far more troublesome to our Nation than is the Military Religious Freedom Foundation which demonstrates its disregard for the very freedom it claims to be defending. I repeat: One person's right to freedom of speech or religion does not negate that same right for another.

Be it on college campus or military base, we must each recognize the corresponding rights of others. A teacher I knew had this sign on the classroom wall: Your right to be disruptive ends where another student's right to a quality education begins!

I urge you, Madam Secretary, to take the lead in correcting this problem. This is not solely in the interest of those who witness a "slap in the face to the POWs that these Missing Man Tables were meant to honor." This issue goes to the very heart of constitutional revisionism by a segment of our society who choose to dishonor not only our POW/MIA veterans, but who would crush the very principles of American freedoms.

On Projection & Democrats

Before we address Kevin Kennedy (Star May 3), it will be helpful if we refresh our memories on the concept of projection.

Not the "images on a silver screen" kind. Rather, the psychological kind. Denial of that which is in and of the self while attributing it to others. Being intolerant while criticizing intolerance in others – that kind of projection!

Whether we use Carl Jung, Sigmund Freud, or Matthew 7:3 as our source, this phenomenon of human behavior is as ubiquitous as mosquitos in today's political world. Kevin has given us a few sterling examples of splinters in my eye, planks in yours (to paraphrase Matthew). Let's notice:

Kevin: . Nothing, that is, except for actions that help to keep its members in power.

Frank: This applies equally to both parties. No sooner is a freshman Congressman elected than he begins fund raising and accumulating sound bites.

See my Star editorial (Congressional Embezzlement) of about this time last year drawing our attention to this still ongoing issue. Also see my response below.

Kevin: So what about the Democrats?

Frank: Yes. What about those Democrats? Try this: Given a Democrat-controlled Congress for 62 of the past 85 years, and given Democratic Party Presidents for 48 of those years, it ought to be easy to see the results of their leadership. Actually, it is easy. All we need to do is compare promises with results. This is what I wrote for another Star editorial. And I supported this with fact, after fact, after fact. Failures in education, bankruptcy in Detroit, economic decline and crime in city after city where Democrat election victories abound. Who is it that wins election after election only to keep its members in power?

Kevin: when that person had no moral compass.

Frank: Moral compass? Let's get serious. Talk about projection! Or don't you believe Hillary had an off-site computer and used it illegally? Do I need to cite for you the list of Federal laws she violated? Have you forgotten that Donna Brazile fed debate questions to candidate Hillary?

Did Hillary return the questions and expose Brazile? And please don't try to convince me Bill Clinton's sexual misconduct inside the Oval Office, on duty, followed by serial lies, followed by impeachment is lesser offense than anything Trump has been accused of! Is there a difference between accused and impeached? One must be careful about that moral compass issue. Some folks do have memories.

Kevin: They care about people born into disadvantaged conditions.

Frank: And the Democrats continue to leave these people in "disadvantaged conditions" even after holding the majority in Congress for those aforementioned 62 years. Check education statistics, crime rates, and employment figures for Detroit, Cleveland, Chicago, Baltimore, and Cleveland. I have done so. I've also verified that the Democrat Party candidates won the majority in each of these cities in the 2016 elections. So, where is the fulfillment of Democrat promises?

And, oh, remember those "Dreamers"? Those "DACA" immigrants? The Democrats have had three opportunities since 2016 to improve their lot. Did they do so?

Kevin: Democrats believe that workers deserve a living wage.

Frank: Have you looked at employment figures recently (4.1%) ? Have you noticed how new (lower) tax rates have increased take-home pay to some 90% of workers. Even CNBC has reported this!

Kevin: Democrats believe that no one should be above the law.

Frank: Here we agree, but that "no one" must include Hillary Clinton for issues I've already cited.

Oh, and about those splinters and planks. Is it possible that Jung and Freud had read Matthew 7:3? Did they use attribution back then?

--30--

On DNA

We've all noticed in recent years a new word, or at least a term, that has entered into our daily vocabulary. It crept into our language almost unnoticed at first. Only certain people spoke of DNA. But it's become ubiquitous thanks mostly to its ability to help solve crimes.

But what is DNA?

Well, the most basic answer is that DNA is a molecule. It's a molecule within a living cell. And that, of course, begs a refresher question. What is a molecule? Well, that's two or more atoms bonded together.

In an effort to keep this uncomplicated so as to enjoy the beauty, let's reduce even the basics to the basics. Let's try this. Suppose we take the letters H and N and O. You'll recognize these as atoms of hydrogen, nitrogen, and oxygen. We've seen these displayed in classrooms. Remember those Periodic Table of Elements charts?

Hydrogen is first on the chart, up in the upper left corner. That's because it weighs the least. These things are arranged by weight. Nitrogen is seventh on the list and oxygen is eighth.

So, if we take two or more of just these three elemental atoms and combine them like a chef does with a recipe, we can come up with some new stuff, new ingredients. So now we're on the path to making DNA.

We start with nothing more than those three letters: H, N, and O. We vary the numbers of each letter and arrange them into patterns to create four new ingredients our chef can use in the recipe. One of those new ingredients has five N's and two H's. Another has two N's along with two H's and two O's. And so it goes. A couple of teaspoons of this. A tablespoon of that. Into this brew our chef adds a pinch of phosphate and a dash of carbon.

Once we've made these four new ingredients, we give them new names. We'll call these new ingredients A, T, G, and C. Then we begin mixing again. Using these four new ingredients, we combine a handful of A's, a cup or so of T's, a jigger of G's, and a baker's dozen of C's. We can make as many varieties of this alphabet soup as we can imagine. Actually, more than we can imagine! We've just made DNA. We took three primary ingredients to make four new things. Then we took those four new things to make DNA.

Okay, we've narrowed the focus a bit. We've done this narrowing so that we'd see the trees before they become obscured by the forest, to misquote an old adage.

Scientists tell us that DNA is a molecule that contains instructions. And this is where my ears perk up a bit. Let's keep that word "instructions" in mind as we examine a couple of remarks from the folks in genome research (www.genome.gov):

Notice this*:

A molecule called deoxyribonucleic acid (DNA) contains the biological instructions that make each species unique.

And this:

DNA contains the instructions needed for each living organism to develop, survive and reproduce. To carry out these functions, DNA sequences are converted into messages that are used to produce proteins, which are the complex molecules that do most of the work in our bodies.

And finally this:

The complete DNA instruction book, or genome, for a human contains about 3 billion of those alphabet soup ATGC "new ingredients" we mentioned earlier, and about 20,000 genes on 23 pairs of chromosomes. But, don't let this escape your attention: that 3 billion refers to a single human cell! That's right! One cell! You and I and seven billion other humans now sharing this planet are each comprised of more than a trillion cells, 15-37 trillion actually. And, yes, each cell contains those aforementioned 3 billion DNA ingredients. I know these numbers are valid. How? Well, I spoke to the young scientist who built the hardware that made it possible to identify and map all this out. It wasn't hard to find him. After all, he is my son.

*The factual information within the preceding three paragraphs, with minor edits for clarity, is from the National Human Genome Research Institute (https://www.genome.gov/).

So now the truth is out. "Scientists" admit that DNA contains "information" and "instructions." The part so many of us often ignore is that where there are instructions, there is an author, an author who creates, who produces, who generates instructions. Instructions do not exist without an author!

So we've taken three ingredients (elements) and with those we varied the number and the pattern of those three to create four new ingredients (molecules). And with those -- again varying only the number and arrangement (pattern, strings) – we've made a new molecule which we've named DNA. And with DNA we create the genetic instructions for every living animal and plant on planet earth. And, oh, let's not leave out the fact that DNA self-replicates! Yes, it copies itself during cell division by splitting its double helix form (akin to a twisted ladder) down the middle and becomes two single strands. "These single strands serve as templates for building two new, double-stranded DNA molecules - each a replica of the original DNA molecule."

Pretty neat trick, eh? Look what we've done starting only with some H, some O, and some N. And let's don't lose sight of something we said on a few lines earlier. And with DNA we create the genetic instructions for every living animal and plant on planet earth. Who can begin to tally up every bush, tree, and flower? Every beast, reptile, and insect? Every fish, bird, and human? Not I. Not you.

But, dear reader, it isn't truly "we" who have done this, right? But it is the most intelligent author this side or any side of eternity. Now please, let's don't kid ourselves. Seven billion human beings – a bit more, actually – live on planet earth. Each person has the aforementioned three billion DNA ingredients per cell. And yet each person is distinguishable, the one from the other, by miniscule variations in that DNA menu. Countless billions of plants. Same A,T,G,C ingredients within who knows how many plant species. Countless billions of animals, insects, and sea creatures. Same A,T,G,C ingredients as the humans and the plants arranged in who knows how many combinations. These numbers are staggering. Literally beyond our ability to calculate.

And you really expect me to believe that all of this "information" and all of these "instructions" are random, are chance, are mere happenstance? And just happen to be self-replicating to accommodate growth and replacement as needed? Get serious!

There is an explanation. There is a Creator. The author of life. And humankind has known this for eons. Among our more recent ancestors who have known this were the 56 men who wrote and signed our nation's Declaration of Independence. (See my article, About Those 56 Men.) These men specifically told us that there is a deity who has established the laws of nature, and this deity is God. They also told us that there is a Creator who created all men. Go ahead. Read it. The Declaration of Independence. Dated July 4, 1776.

But in recent years we have among us many, perhaps millions, who choose to disbelieve the very words our founding fathers wrote. They think we humans have grown beyond, have out-smarted, those men. These modern humans would have us believe humankind capable of surpassing even the Author of Life. Those who believe such are in for a major surprise! Please notice this (a):

Foolish by nature were all who were in ignorance of God, and who from the good things seen did not succeed in knowing the one who is, and from studying the works did not discern the artisan; Instead either fire, or wind, or the swift air, or the circuit of the stars, or the mighty water, or the luminaries of heaven, the governors of the world, they considered gods. Now if out of joy in their beauty they thought them gods, let them know how far more excellent is the Lord than these; for the original source of beauty fashioned them. Or if they were struck by their might and energy, let them realize from these things how much more powerful is the one who made them. For from the greatness and the beauty of created things their original author, by analogy, is seen. But yet, for these the blame is less; For they have gone astray perhaps, though they seek God and wish to find him. For they search busily among his works, but are distracted by what they see, because the things seen are fair. But again, not even these are pardonable. For if they so far succeeded in knowledge that they could speculate about the world, how did they not more quickly find its Lord?

Another author put it a bit more succinctly (b):

The wrath of God is indeed being revealed from heaven against every impiety and wickedness of those who suppress the truth by their wickedness. For what can be known about God is evident to them, because God made it evident to them. Ever since the creation of the world, his invisible attributes of eternal power and divinity have been able to be understood and perceived in what he has made. As a result, they have no excuse; for although they knew God they did not accord him glory as God or give him thanks. Instead, they became vain in their reasoning, and their senseless minds were darkened. While claiming to be wise, they became fools and exchanged the glory of the immortal God for the likeness of an image of mortal man or of birds or of four-legged animals or of snakes. They exchanged the truth of God for a lie and revered and worshiped the creature rather than the creator, who is blessed forever.

David, father of King Solomon, said much the same yet still more concisely: The heavens declare the glory of God; the skies proclaim the work of his hands.

So, go ahead. Allow yourself to believe that everything from DNA to the galaxies of the cosmos is naught but random chaotic chance. The day will come when you and I will meet that Author of those "instructions." And when we do, I'm not at all certain we'll be able to convince Him we are His equal.

Notes:

If this had been a textbook, we could have used 25¢ vocabulary words such as nucleobase, nucleotide, adenosine triphosphate, heterocyclic aromatic ring, not to mention phosphates, a sugar called deoxyribose, and four nitrogenous bases. We could have explained every detail of DNA and its resulting components, genes, chromosomes, and cells. If we had done so, would you have kept reading?

I doubt if I would have. Besides, my goal here was to remain under 2,000 words. Goal achieved.

By the way, those two Scriptural quotes were from New American Bible, Revised Edition, March 9, 2011:

Wisdom 13: 1-9 (This book is not contained in all Bible editions).
Romans 1: 18-25, with v. 24 deleted because it introduced a theme inconsistent with this article.

-30-

On Spectroscopy & Creation

Excuse the pun here, but I am inclined to reflect upon the matter of creation. You may have noticed this in some of my other writings. The pun will become more evident as we proceed, but for me, the who, the what, the how, and the why of creation are captivating topics.

Not long ago, I found myself attempting to understand DNA. As concisely as possible, I reduced the topic to this:

> DNA begins with three elements. These we combine in different numbers and patterns to form molecules. So, starting with only hydrogen, oxygen, and nitrogen, we vary the numbers and the pattern of these to create four new ingredients (molecules). And with those four molecules -- again varying only the number and arrangement into patterns and strings -- we make every living animal and plant on planet earth.

Neat trick, eh? Later, we'll clarify what we mean by "we." But for now, visualize a chef. He uses three primary ingredients to make four appetizers. Then he combines the appetizers to make four entrées. Finally, with the entrées, he produces an infinite number of meals.

Now just about the time I thought I had clarified the DNA topic, a flash of light impelled me to examine spectroscopy. Might this *scientific tool of analysis* lead me to a more complete understanding of creation? After all, DNA has revealed itself to be *a complete set of instructions used to make every cell of every living animal and plant on earth.* And where there are instructions, there is one who authors those instructions. So, what might spectroscopy reveal about this author?

In its most elemental terms, spectroscopy is a study of how light interacts with matter. It'll help here if we begin by refreshing our memories on a handful of terms:

- Light. Most often when we speak of light, we are referring to visible light - daylight, sunlight, light produced by a lightbulb, the opposite of dark, and so forth. But, in fact, visible light is only a small part of something much larger. That "something" is electromagnetic radiation.
- Electromagnetic radiation. This is energy that is all around us and takes many forms, such as radio waves, microwaves, X-rays and gamma rays. For the sake of convenience, we most often see this depicted as a horizontal line with short "waves" at one end and long "waves" at the other. In classical physics, we speak of a flow of energy at the universal speed of light through free space or through a material.
- Matter. The "stuff" of the universe.
- Spectroscope. We are more familiar with *telescope* or *microscope*. This "scope" is an apparatus, or tool, used for observing and measuring properties of light. A Spectrometer *measures* and a spectrograph *records* the information.

With this we can see that spectroscopy uses these tools to study the interaction between light and matter.

Are you beginning to see the light?
In another book I wrote about "light" this way:

> In the book of Genesis, God said, *"Let there be light," and there was light.*
>
> It is also reasonable to conclude that "light," having been created, has the same properties and characteristics as does "light" as we know it today. Given this, then, the presence of "light," being one part, or segment, of the "electromagnetic spectrum," indicates the presence also of the remainder of the electromagnetic spectrum. Hence, the creation of "light" - also known as "radiant energy" - included all other forms of radiant energy. Thus, gamma rays, x-rays, ultraviolet radiation, light, infrared radiation, microwaves, and radio waves were at once created with "*Let there be light.*"

So, let's get back to our topic of light interacting with matter.

Joe Scientist stumbles upon a piece of stuff. He wants to know what it is. So, he zaps it with a bit of radiant energy (light). The stuff responds. As radiation strikes or passes through the sample, it might be absorbed, reflected, or refracted (change direction). Aha! Joe Scientist has identified the "stuff."

But how? How does Joe distinguish between one kind of stuff from another?

This is where it gets interesting. This is where that "author" reenters the picture. Now please don't try to convince me that all this is random. It most certainly is not. Not chance. Not happenstance. It is design!

You see, it turns out that each and every piece of "stuff" on this planet or out in space - atoms, elements organic, inorganic - responds to that zap in its own unique way. Here, even scientists, be it Joe or any of his colleagues, agree on these terms:

- Discrete
- Distinct
- Unique
- One of a kind
- Unlike anything else

So, whether Joe Scientist or Einstein himself zaps a piece of "stuff" the result will be the same. The stuff will be identified. No guesswork.

Astronomers can identify what kinds of stuff are in stars from the lines and waves they find in the star's spectrum. Analytical chemists can determine the content and purity of a sample as well as its molecular structure. Do fingerprints come to mind?
Looking back, now, to what we have learned about DNA, we see that each and every living plant and animal has a unique, one-of-a-kind, set of "instructions" allowing us to identify the one from the other.

And now we see that each and every atom, element, and molecule of "stuff" has its own one-of-a-kind response to light, whether visible or invisible.

And you want to believe there is no author? I don't find it hard to believe. But what I do find hard to believe is that modern science gives us clear evidence, and still many of us choose to disbelieve. Odd that the 56 men who signed the *Declaration of Independence* specifically told us that there is a deity who has established the laws of nature, and this deity is God. They also told us that there is a Creator who created all men. Go ahead. Read it. The *Declaration of Independence.* Dated July 4, 1776.
At what point, then, in our Nation's history did so many of us decide that we are more intelligent than the Creator who authored life's instruction book (DNA) and made each and every bit of "stuff" such that it displays its identity for us if we but shine light upon it?

And you still want to believe there is no author?

-30-

On Gender Identity

Dear Beloved Granddaughter, what we have here is my response to your online Title IX posting. Please don't remove me from the family roster. I love you and all of my grandchildren. ....

When addressing issues of gender, one must take care to distinguish between types of feeling. There is the realm of emotional feeling and the realm of somatic feeling. These are distinct types of feeling, yet the two often exist in a symbiotic relationship not unlike the double helix of DNA.

So, am I suggesting that gender is nothing but a matter of feelings? Certainly not. Read on.

Discussions of gender in today's politically-charged arena becomes a hot-button issue largely because too many of us fail to do what successful football coaches do. Focus on the basics.

We must first focus on two words: *being* and *doing*. Being is a matter of biology. Doing is a matter of choice. We'll return to this.

We must also focus on three classical categories (or types) of love. Eros, Philia, and Agape. (Yes, I know that *Psychology Today* has expanded the list to seven. But if you look closely, the additional four are but variations of the basic three. Of the classic three you'll readily recognize the distinction between eros and philia. Agape, on the other hand, is less frequently encountered. Here I prefer the

Thomas Aquinas rendering: *to will the good of the other.* Again, we'll return to this.

A third topic we must incorporate into the discussion is that of rights. *Rights* has become the focal point of current controversy. But before I offer my thoughts on the rights topic, allow me first to step aside in the realm of personal. This will give you a more complete idea of what I bring to the table.

First, I have lived and worked side-by-side with homosexual men. I knew they were homosexual, and they knew that I knew. It wasn't an issue. I respected them and they me. Matters of gender preference did not influence our working and living relationships. Early in my Air Force career – I would have been a bit younger than 20 at the time – I defended two such men when they were being investigated for removal from the Air Force. They continued their careers.

Over the years, I have kept my eyes, ears, and brain open in the event some research might eventually answer the essential how, why, and whom questions. To the best of my present knowledge those questions remain unanswered.

But to someone who commented on your online post, I can with near certainty rule out her nematodes and Klinefelter concerns. In the case of nematodes, the hundreds of cells associated with their reproductive systems does not imply that those cells develop into one, another, or multiple genders. Nematodes have remained a structurally simple organism whose chief function is to enrich soil. As for Klinefelter, no evidence to date has surfaced that this random error in cell division is anything but that – a random error. When seeking cause-and-effect relationships, we must always be open to both *either-or* and also to *both-and* propositions. Yes, some of the Klinefelter characteristics do reveal what some might call feminine traits. But there are many homosexual persons who exhibit few, if any, of the Klinefelter indications.

That *random error*, however, does offer me an opportunity to venture into a bit of a segue into two closely related topics. Don't panic. I'm going to mention the Bible here. It's not a snake. It has never bitten anyone. Not even a college professor.

As an aside, I must fess up. Until the age of about 60, I had not read the Bible. Oh, a phrase or two here and there. But not truly read the Bible. That was an error. But now I do. And I love it. At age 75 I cannot imagine not reading the Bible. Daily. So, yes, in portions of this discussion I will make reference to or quote from the Bible. Hang in there. Open your mind and your heart – as I have finally done – and you'll find it won't harm you!

The Bible tells us God created mankind in the image and likeness of God. And, yes, I do believe this. But let's let that discussion rest upon the table-top for the moment. What I wish to focus on are the words *image* and *likeness*.

Both *image* and *likeness* are but a reflection of, but not the substance of, the object itself. Hence, we humans are not clones of our creator. Nor are we our own creator. We have flaws and imperfections. Some of us are born blind, or deaf, or both. Helen Keller comes to mind. Despite lacking both sight and hearing, she became a college graduate and an author. I remain both fascinated and mystified with her. (As an aside, consider her quote: *The best and most beautiful things in the world cannot be seen or even touched - they must be felt with the heart.*

I digress, but only a little. The topic was flaws and imperfections. When it comes to the homosexual topic, I have come to prefer a term with fewer negative connotations. I use *variant* where others might choose *abnormal* if not something more derogatory. Hence, I have no basis to feel superior to a person who has a variant that I may not share.

Now, allow me to return to a topic touched upon earlier. Love. Here I will draw upon excerpts from something I wrote a few years ago for your cousin Lance. Bear with me, please. I'm convinced you'll discern the connection with our present topic. You, Beloved Granddaughter, will readily recognize the rationale here. And whether we speak of love coming from God or of love from and with a human, this remains true:

Love does not and cannot exist in a vacuum. Love requires reciprocity. The reciprocity of love is like an oval. The giving is complete only with the receiving. The receiving responds with giving. The giver becomes the recipient who again becomes the giver. From this, it is clear that love is "other-directed." And this is the distinction between love and self-satisfaction. From this, you can perceive that the pursuit of self-satisfaction interrupts the cyclical nature of love. There can be no reciprocity when self-satisfaction is the goal. This is likewise true in the physical realm.

Physical intimacy is an ingredient of love, an expression of love. And as with the "reciprocal process" of love, physical intimacy relies upon that same "other-directed" nature of love. When the emphasis is upon self-satisfaction rather than mutual-satisfaction, the cycle of reciprocity is interrupted and love falters.

You'll understand, Beloved Granddaughter, that I am not suggesting that homosexuals are incapable of experiencing this sort of reciprocity in love, whether with God or with another human being. But I am saying – as I suggested at the beginning of this discourse – that love is not limited to *feeling*. Sacrifice, an essential ingredient, is the *sine qua non* of love. And where such sacrifice is absent so is *to will the good of the other*. True for homosexuals. True for heterosexuals.

I have long been grappling with this issue. And recently I have even entered into debate with Christians who themselves often err when they comment on what the Bible says on the topic. Please read carefully what I wrote to a professor of religion, and be alert to <u>what I do not say</u>:

> But perhaps the most important thing Jesus says with respect to the topic of homosexuality is this: "Do not think that I have come to abolish the Law or the Prophets; I have not come to abolish them but to fulfill them." He added, "... not the smallest letter, not the least stroke of a pen, will by any means disappear from the Law until everything is accomplished."

Now what "Law" do we suppose Jesus is speaking about? Well, that would be the first five books of the Bible, the Torah. One of these is Leviticus within which chapters 18 and 20 make clear what Jesus and His Father think of "practicing" homosexuality. And for those who think Leviticus is only for Levite priests, look again. The Apostle Paul - whom Jesus not so gently recruited - offers the same advice in Romans 1.

So that I might better grasp what God offers us from Genesis to Revelation, I prefer to read the whole Bible, not solely the parts that conform to my fondest desires for humanity. You have told our readers that Jesus "never speaks about" homosexual practice. But you err! He does so in Matthew 5 which I quoted above. True, Jesus does not utter the words "homosexual, homosexuality, or orientation." But He does clearly tell us that He neither abolishes nor changes the Law. And you as a Bible scholar surely know the "Law" he speaks of. And you know where to find this verse:

"'*Do not have sexual relations with a man as one does with a woman; that is detestable.*"

So, yes, Jesus does speak "of" homosexuality. This is not manipulation of the Bible, Professor. And, yes, those texts are relevant today, contrary to your statement otherwise.

Do you believe Jesus errs when he says *"... not the smallest letter, not the least stroke of a pen, will by*

> *any means disappear from the Law until everything is accomplished*"? Do you believe everything has been accomplished?
>
> Finally, my article did not say Jesus abhors the homosexual person, or, for that matter, the adulterous person. You and I both know what He does abhor. Actions which preclude our eternal union with Him. He wants us. He wants us to want Him. We must all want Him enough to sacrifice that which He abhors. For homosexuals that sacrifice is an act of love He will not forget.

And here, before we move to a related topic (that of rights), allow me to explain two reasons why – to quote the text – God finds*: sexual relations with a man as one does with a woman; that is detestable.* For starters, He finds such an act *detestable* because it corrupts a gift He created and gave to us. The human body He gave us was designed for one purpose, and some humans choose to use it for another.

There is a second reason He detests *homosexual activity.* (Again <u>notice what I am not saying</u>, specifically the person. He created the person. He loves the person. He wants eternal union with the person. He does not detest the person.) That second reason is based upon another feature of the human body. This feature is one many of us seldom give a thought to. Our bodies do not exist in complete solitude. Each human also has its own spirit. Some of us are aware of that spirit. Others are not. It nevertheless remains a fact. And, also a fact, each of us has been gifted with the Holy Spirit. Be kind enough, Beloved

Granddaughter, not too soon to erect a wall here. But do consider this feature of our human bodies:

> *We have a body of flesh but a mind of spirit.*
> *Do you not know that your bodies are temples of the Holy Spirit, who is in you, whom you have received from God? You are not your own;*
> *Now the body is not for fornication, but for the Lord; and the Lord for the body.*

I could offer other such quotes. But these will suffice. And let's be realistic. If you choose not to believe these, the likelihood is not great you would choose to believe others.

Now we come to the conflict between feelings and rights. And here my views are pragmatic in nature and based upon my own experiences in the public-school classroom. In 1985, when I began teaching German and English to 6th, 7th, 8th, and 9th grade students, I had a sign clearly posted in my classroom. It read: "*Your right to be disruptive ends where your classmates' right to a quality education begins.*" That same principle applies to today's debates over gender equality rights.

We cannot, and should not, allow the *feelings* of the few, to override the *rights* of the many. I do not wish to be insensitive, but neither do I wish to be nonsensical. It is not feelings that determine gender in human beings. We must keep that fact in mind if we hope to avoid the chaos which disrupts the education of the many. Yes, I have empathy for the girl who feels she is male. That is a struggle no one should have to endure. Yet it is a personal struggle. It is not the obligation of city, county, state, or federal government agencies - or school districts -- to spend taxpayer funds, time, or other resources in an effort to address the "feelings" of those who wish to be, or feel like, another gender. Yes, taxpayers are a major factor here. That is why each case must be addressed locally. Public funds are required to alter, renovate, or replace public buildings. This is true regardless of one's interest in gender rights issues.

Now, open your mind wide enough to allow me a word on same-gender marriage. Neither the word *marriage* nor even the concept of marriage are to be found written in the Constitution. The clear evidence, then, is that marriage is not an event over which the federal government has any jurisdiction. Marriage is and remains a spiritually-based sacrament involving a life-long covenant between one man and one woman. This is <u>not</u> to imply that same-gender unions should not qualify for the same legal benefits due all others.

Same-gender marriage, then, is a matter to be decided at the local level and solely by the participating parties, including, if so desired, any ecclesiastical participation. Same-gender couples need to recognize that the absence of such language within the Constitution is not an accident. Some things are meant to be accomplished at the local level.

But we live in a time when nonsense prevails. We have U.S. Supreme Court judges who have twisted the Constitution of the United States into a pretzel. Did these justices not receive a basic education in biology as well as law? Humans are not ovoviviparous. We are not gastropods or other forms of hermaphrodite biological specimens. We are mammals. Placental mammals. Our females nourish their young within the womb. Females have specific reproductive organs. Males have others. Male and female external genital organs differ. Basic biology. As a result of these differences, male-male and female-female sexual union is not natural. It cannot result, for example, in natural birth.

Ah, and there it is. That word "natural." Our courts, our news media, and certain agenda-driven agencies have heaped nonsense upon nonsense until we have blinded ourselves with feelings. We no longer pay heed to the natural. This despite the fact that our very forefathers, those who gave this nation its Constitution, were of such education that they knew, and took into consideration, nature - the natural.

Consider the 56 American founding leaders who wrote about "*the Laws of Nature and of Nature's God.*" These words were part of the Declaration of Independence. It is inconceivable that these men would have been unaware of the basics of biology! I certainly doubt they would have ever imagined a time when our nation would be struggling with such issues as whether a girl should be using a boys' school bathroom, or whether a male should be marrying a male.

And now, finally, to that Title IX issue which was the central issue of your posting. That original legislation was written (1972) at a time long before the terms *sexual orientation* and *gender identity* were part of the nation's vocabulary.

The discrimination issue driving the legislation had to do solely with gender parity with respect to school activities and facilities. In brief, girls wanted (and, yes, deserved) equality with boys - level playing field, so to speak. The emphasis was chiefly, if not solely, with respect to sports. And, yes, there currently are "proposed revisions" being discussed. So, you are well advised to speak out on the issue. *Proposed*, however is not the same as *completed.*

So, Beloved Granddaughter, I hope you have taken the time to read all of this. I do not expect you to agree with all that I have written here. But I do hope that from this you will recognize that not all of those are homophobic who object to some of the gender-movement social agenda. We may object for reasons not at all lacking in tolerance and love. My own objections - as I hope you have discerned within this discourse - are based upon love for the person and respect for the rights of all.

Hoping that you have not yet decided to hate me, I'll add these two related thoughts from other recent products of my writing. This is discernably related to what we are here considering.

....

We slid to where we are today when we began to ignore, and to willfully redefine, how human life begins. Understanding the truth is not actually all that complicated. Reduced to the basics, the formula is this: sperm + ovum = human cell. We call this process fertilization. And once fertilization takes place what follows is a steady increase in numbers of cells and types of cells.

I refreshed my memory a day or two ago, and came up with this summary:

A fertilized human cell begins to divide repeatedly. The rest of the process is numbers and types. As cells divide the number of cells increases. Then cells begin to differentiate, different types of cells result. These different types will become different organs. So, at the instant of fertilization (sperm + egg = cell), the number and types of cells begin to increase. The simple term for this process is growth.

Those two key words "process" and "growth" are central to understanding the truth about human life. Life itself is a process. Beginning, maturation, end. That's the process in the simplest of terms.

Now consider "growth." That which grows has life. True for humans, true for animals, true for plants. Stated another way, if it's growing it's alive. If it's alive, it has life. Now returning to that fertilized human cell, consider this. Given roughly 270 days, the number and types of human cells will have grown to the point at which life within the womb is ready to commence to life outside the womb. So, the only differences between that first fertilized cell and the human being which emerges at birth are time and growth.

Until recently, some 55 million abortions in our nation have been shrouded with the lies which began with the "What we call it" game. We have allowed our consciences to be soothed by hiding behind terms like fetus, embryo, and abortion. Only those who make the effort to consult a dictionary will come to notice the truth. A fetus is a human life. An embryo is a human life. An abortion is the termination of a human life. It's that simple. The rest is choice.

--30--

On Socialism

An Meine Enkelinnen (To My granddaughters)

I am compelled by the tenor of our times. I am compelled by the fact that you are flesh of my flesh, bone of my bone. I am compelled because time is precious. I am compelled because I love you.

I must share with you or forever regret that I failed to do so. First, I must remind you of my bona fides, that is, the documentary evidence of my legitimacy, my credentials. Your professors call this Curriculum Vitae. It's how they explain the alphabet soup they place following their names.

Most professors offer you the vegetables of their personal garden plots. Doctoral dissertations. Masters theses. Few, if any, of these academics can match my bona fides.
My sources are what I have seen and experienced, in situ, that is, in and within its original place. My sources are street-level, nitty-gritty, real people who lived with and during socialism, communism, and national socialism. I spoke, and still speak, face-to-face with these people. I dined with them. I lodged with them. I went to their weddings and their funerals. I wept with them and laughed with them. I went with them into their churches, their schools. I worked and sweat with them. Picked mushrooms in the forests with them. I shopped with them. Played cards and chess with them. I learned their language, their history, their culture.

So, damn it, when I tell you what I know about socialism, communism, and national socialism, listen to me!

Your professors can lecture you on Engels, Marx, Hegel, Trotsky, and Lenin. That's their turf. I, on the other hand, offer you a reality check. Consider this: if I throw an apple to break a window, does that rob all apples of nutrients? Ought we campaign to remove all apples from the grocer's shelves? Alas, this is the flaw in the writings of Engels, Marx, and the rest. I won't argue whether these scholars observed abuse at the hands of some they called capitalists. But we don't behead a sick hen in the attempt to cure her! At least not if we wish to continue having eggs. This is likewise the very illogic indulged in by many who today call themselves progressives or liberals and seek to cure our ills with socialism. They speak of utopian dreams. I reduce those dreams to hard facts.

Let's start with hard fact number one. Let's say I apply to an apple a sticky-label reading "banana." Does the apple become a banana? Of course not. And the same is true with the label "socialist" and, for that matter, "communist." If I label an autocracy as socialist, it remains an autocracy. Likewise true for a communist state labeled "Democratic Republic."

Have I ever seen a communist country bearing the label "Democratic Republic"? Well, yes, as a matter of fact, I have! I have even traveled to and within such a place. The German Democratic Republic. That happens to be the place your grandmother Josefine was born.
Problem is, only one word of that label was true. It was German. But it most assuredly was not democratic. Nor was it a republic.

The point here is that just as we cannot judge a book by its cover, neither can we judge a country by its label. We have to examine how it behaves and what it does. Only then can we decide what it is.

Speaking of labels and terminology, stop for a moment and reflect on these questions:

What is the difference between an oligarchy and an autocracy?
Who has greater prestige - the proletariat or the bourgeoisie?
How does socialism differ from communism?
Is one better off being an Apparatchik or being a Politburo member?
Is the United States a democracy? Or, is our country a republic?
What is the meaning of the suffix "cracy"?

If you can answer these questions with ease, thank your high school teacher or your college professor. If, on the other hand, you struggle with any of these, your professors may not be worth their paychecks.

Now, let's get back to labels. And some facts.

Russia was not a communist country. But it was an oligarchy hiding behind the label of communism. Had it been communist, it would have been a classless society. But it wasn't, and still isn't. Those at the helm of leadership and most of their apparatchiks had privileges not available to the rest of society. They had special stores where they could buy Western products. They had private country villas (dacha -- a country house or cottage). They drove quality cars – the Volga rather than the Lada. The working-class rode -- and still ride -- street cars, buses, and subways.

Definitely not classless. The oligarchs lived a lifestyle several notches above that of the commoners. "But they have elections," you might say. True, but their elections are like crystal selling for the price of diamond. Later we'll examine detailed facts about elections in Russia, Cuba and Iran. But for now, ponder, please, on this:

2018 - Vladimir Putin, President (Prime Minister is Dmitry Medvedev)
2012-2018 Vladimir Putin, President (Prime Minister is Dmitry Medvedev)
2008-2012 Vladimir Putin, Prime Minister (President is Dmitry Medvedev)
2000-2008 Vladimir Putin, President

This exercise of musical chairs is oligarchy at its most brazen. And what your professors likely do not tell you is this: Executive power in each of these political dances always remained with Putin. When Medvedev was president, the office was ceremonial head of state, while the office of prime minister under Putin wielded executive power.

What I most hope you will discern is how people who seek power will abuse labels – sort of the wolf in sheep's clothing – to gain control over others. Hopefully, once adequately informed, you can avoid buying into the deceit offered by those who choose to ignore, or hide, reality.

So let's take a closer look at elections. What I am about to reveal to you is true for Russia, China, and Cuba to mention only three. But it also is true for Iran. Iran? Yes, but the labels are different. A hammer remains a hammer even when it has a religious label!
I don't wish for this essay to grow to the 560 pages of Marx's Capital, so I'll be concise. I'll focus on common denominators to put it arithmetical terms. Let's start with a few quotes from sources you might recognize. These folks are telling you what I - as noted earlier - already know because I have seen and witnessed these events over a period of years.

First this from Cuba's most recent election:

"If the Cuban Communist Party — the only party allowed to participate in elections under the one-party regime...." From <https://www.nytimes.com/2018/02/26/opinion/cuba-castro-election-democracy.html>

"The 86-year-old Castro will remain head of the Communist Party, which is designated by the constitution as 'the superior guiding force of society and the state.' As a result, he will still be the most powerful person in Cuba for the time being." From <http://www.chicagotribune.com/news/nationworld/ct-cuba-presidential-election-20180418-story.html>

"As in Cuba's legislative elections, all of the leaders selected Wednesday were picked by a government-appointed commission. Ballots offer only the option of approval or disapproval and candidates generally receive more than 95 percent of the votes in their favor."

From http://www.chicagotribune.com/news/nationworld/ct-cuba-presidential-election-20180418-story.html>

And now this from Iran's most recent election:

> "The Supreme Leader -- currently an ultra-conservative cleric named Ayatollah Ali Khamenei -- helps appoint the Guardian Council, an unelected panel of conservatives that decides who gets to run for president (and who doesn't). Many popular reformist candidates have been disqualified from running in recent elections." From <https://www.cnn.com/2017/05/16/middleeast/iran-election-beginners-guide/index.html>
>
> "But not everyone is allowed to take part. The guardian council, a powerful body of six clergymen and six jurists, vets each candidacy. Political competence and loyalty to the fundamental principles of the Islamic republic and its religion are among the main issues considered by the council. This year, out of more than 1,600 who applied to run, only six candidates were accepted."
> From
> <https://www.theguardian.com/world/2017/may/16/iran-presidential-elections-everything-you-need-to-know>

Not too difficult to spot common denominators, eh? Single party, government appointed commission, only "vetted" candidates permitted. And, yes, the labels vary, but this process is the same for Russia and China.

Do you really need arithmetic now to grasp why candidates in these -and other such - countries receive 95% of votes cast. (Okay, sometimes for appearance sake we'll see only 75% or so. That usually means that only 75% voted, not that 25% voted for another candidate. After all, there was no other candidate.)

Now let's shift our attention to economics.

You may notice I'll be making little distinction here between communism and socialism when it comes to economics. That's because it's sort of a Fifty Shades of Grey thing. What one calls state ownership of the means of production, the other calls social ownership and workers' self-management of the means of production. With Cuba, it's blatantly black-and-white. Not much grey. Here is how the New York Times puts it:

"The Cuban military, through its conglomerate Gaesa, owns the vast majority of firms that operate engaged [sic] in trade, from hotels to foreign exchange houses to ports, which gives it control of up to 60 percent of incoming hard currency. Any economic reformer knows that breaking a monopoly is difficult, even more so if the monopolist also holds power over arms and intelligence. Cuba's military is committed to not just one-party rule, but also, it seems, to one-firm economics. And because Cuba's economy is so closed, the private sector is small and weak."

Just for emphasis if not for clarification, I would add this: Cuba's military and Cuba's communist party is a symbiotic relationship so tightly bound it could pass for a Möbius strip.

But let's get to the point here. When we speak of socialism/communism, we must clearly discern its effect on a nation's economy. Otherwise, we are simply fooling ourselves. Or, we are allowing ourselves to be fooled. Take your pick.

Here the Chicago Tribune puts it well:

> "He (Castro) has failed to fix the generally unproductive and highly subsidized state-run businesses that, along with a Soviet-model bureaucracy, employ three of every four Cubans. State salaries average $30 a month, leaving workers struggling to feed their families, and often dependent on corruption or remittances from relatives overseas."

Don't allow the arithmetic to slip past you here. A whopping 75% of Cubans earn an average of $30 a month. Keep that in mind as adherents of socialism in our country block your view with labels!

Speaking of $30 a month, allow me to share with you how and where I learned about the "benefits" of socialism. In this case "democratic socialism." That's a blended system. Seen in such places as Sweden, Norway, and Denmark.

So, what do I know about Socialism in Denmark? Well, I lived and worked side by side with two Danes for a full year. In a place called Thule. Owing to periods of 24-hour darkness and others of 24-hour daylight, there's plenty of time for chatting. Their names were Michael Lindblad and Lars Norgard and what they had to say astounded me, then and still does today.

Unlike the Americans who spent a year at Thule (a U.S. Air Force Base not far from geographic North Pole, which itself was not far from North Magnetic Pole) many Danes remained living and working at Thule for 10, 15, or 20 years before heading back to Denmark.

One day I asked Michael and Lars why they stayed so long at Thule. They explained it was because of taxes. As long as they worked at Thule, their income was 100% tax-free. And that made a lot more sense when they added the rest of the story. Danes back home paid taxes of 60% on their income. Sixty-percent! Reverse that and you'll see that Danes receive only 40% of their income. For every 10 hours of work they'd receive 4 hours of pay.

Do I need to tell you more about Socialism? I will, because there's much more to tell. But keep this image in mind. It'll be useful as we progress.

Progress. That's an interesting word. It can be a noun. It can also be a verb. Notice the shift in sound. What we need to notice is that progress, in the sense of productivity, is what suffers first and most when socialism (or unions) change the emphasis of a company from creating and producing widgets to creating and fostering a social agenda for the workers.

Here's what happens. A company is founded by one or more investors. These folks invest cash to launch the company. They do so in a quest for profit. That's not evil, by the way. Especially when investors use profit to build more companies. More workers have jobs.

Okay, so that's a brief primer on free enterprise, also known as capitalism. (Investors put up the capital. They also shoulder the risk of failure.) Investors fund research and development. When it's time to produce widgets (my term for any product), the company hires people. Then the buzz begins. Investors purchase raw materials. Transportation enters the picture. Company work staff assembles and finishes the widgets. Transportation reenters the picture. Move the widgets from the factory to the marketplace.

And so it goes. Until? Well, until we look at the impact of socialism - by whatever label. Now, don't get me wrong here. I am not saying that labor and management in free enterprise should not identify and address issues to improve the workplace and the workforce. That's an obvious win-win for all concerned. The issue is a matter of responsible balance. In most successful businesses, this practice is already well-established.

The impact of socialism has already been partially addressed. Earlier I mentioned what suffers first and most when socialism (or unions) change the emphasis of a company. There is a shift from creating and producing widgets to creating and fostering a social agenda for the workers. In my Air Force career, we spoke of "time over target," and in my teaching career we spoke of "time on task." Both of these referred to the amount of time devoted to a particular task. (Though the Air Force term could also refer to time-of-arrival over target.) So, let's focus on widgets and the time necessary to produce them.

Here, the number 86,400 comes to mind. That's the total number of seconds in a day. Now let's reduce that to a standard 8-hour shift at work in the factory. Now we're down to 28,800. That's the number of seconds workers in any factory have to produce widgets. That looks like a hefty number of time until we reduce it to minutes. We have but 480 minutes in that 8-hour shift to produce widgets.

This makes it easier to see the impact of socialism in the factory environment. The first thing we lose is time-on-task. That translates to fewer widgets. And that, in turn, translates to fewer sales. You see where this is going, right?

Socialism (and our own labor unions) bring about a second reduction in both productivity and profit owing to the issue of work incentives. But before departing too far from that word profit, let us keep in mind that it is profit in free enterprise business that allows owner-investors to fund growth in the company. Often, this is overlooked by critics of capitalism.

Now, returning to work and work incentives, allow me to remind you that my source materials for the following are both my own personal experience (labor union) together with the experience of family, friends, and co-workers I mentioned above.

Labor unions reduce productivity in this way: Labor and management negotiate to establish a quota. Let's say 15 widgets produced per hour per employee. An employee – eager to achieve – produces 20 widgets per hour. This employee will be severely ostracized, cold-shouldered, shunned by fellow employees and especially by the union. Why? First, because the overachiever makes fellow employees appear to be laggards. But more important – to the union – is that owner-management would be encouraged to raise the quota having seen the achievement. But union leaders do not want a quota raised. Why? They want owner-management to hire additional employees. Why? Each union employee pays monthly dues to the union.

We'll return to the effects of Socialism upon a nation's economy following this brief segue into labor union realities. Looking solely at the AFL-CIO (a federation of some 56 unions), here are some revealing facts which illustrate the above "why" questions. This federation of unions:

Has 12,475,220 members.
Collects member monthly dues of $112,276,800.
That's an annual sum of $1,743,321,600.
Pays its top 10 employees an annual sum of $2,413,604.00.
Contributes $1,562,358,840.00 in election donations.
Of these election donations 93.5% goes to Democrat Party.

(I did not "invent" these facts. They come directly from this web page – https://www.unionfacts.com/union/AFL-CIO).

And, please, don't overlook this rather salient detail: That annual sum of employee dues paid is $1.7 billion that would have gone into employee paychecks and into the economy had it not gone to the union! And that's just AFL-CIO money. If you have a bit more curiosity than a lizard has fur, you might ferret out an aggregate figure for all union dues. I'd be impressed!

Now let's review those "why" questions:

But union leaders do not want a quota raised. Why? They want owner-management to hire additional employees. Why? Each union employee pays monthly dues to the union.

With this as a means of comparison, not to dollar figures, but to the effects of socialism upon a nation's economy, let's dig deeper.

While I know from personal observation and family discussions what follows, I'll be quoting from a clearly written article. I'll source the article for you at the end of this section. You might want to read "the rest of the story" to quote Paul Harvey. But let's begin with these nuggets:

> Socialism creates a strong incentive to shirk.
> Socialism penalizes industrious behavior.
> Socialism rewards sloth and indolence.
> Socialism promises prosperity and freedom. But the incentives created by socialism place it in a dilemma. If the workers are allowed to remain "free," they will not produce. To stimulate production, they must be

> denied their freedom. Thus, socialism cannot achieve both prosperity and freedom. Usually it results in neither.

This anecdote reveals the conundrum:

Assume that an individual, Clem, is a member of a socialist commune. Assume that there are 1,000 members of the commune and that the output is divided equally among the members. (For the sake of simplicity, we will ignore matters such as capital investment.) Let's say that the production of the commune totals 100,000 bushels of wheat a year, or an average of 100 bushels per member. At a price of, say, $5.00 per bushel total receipts for the commune are $500,000, or $500 per member. The question is: How is Clem likely to behave? Will he work hard? Will he shirk?

Let's assume that Clem is both naturally industrious and socially conscientious. He is concerned about the overall good of the commune. As a result, Clem works very hard and increases his production from 100 to 150 bushels of wheat a year. This increases the annual output of the commune from 100,000 to 100,050 bushels. At $5.00 per bushel the income of the commune increases from $500,000 to $500,250. Since total income is divided equally among the members, the income of each member rises from $500 to $500.25 a year. Thus, because of his extra work Clem's production increased 50 per cent. But his income increased by a mere 25¢ or by 0.05 per cent. Moreover, the income of the other 999 members also increased by 25¢ even though they did not work any harder and their productivity did not increase.

Clearly, Clem's activities benefited everyone in the commune except himself. Everyone else had his income increase without increasing his work. But Clem's income increased only 25¢ despite increasing his work load by 50 per cent. While the benefits of the extra production were diffused throughout the commune, the costs were concentrated on Clem.

Poor Clem! He's no better off than the American union laborer who gets ostracized for exceeding his quota. Hmmm.

But thanks to Clem, we are now in a better position to understand today's Cuba and this quote:

He (Castro) has failed to fix the generally unproductive and highly subsidized state-run businesses that, along with a Soviet-model bureaucracy, employ three of every four Cubans. State salaries average $30 a month, leaving workers struggling to feed their families, and often dependent on corruption or remittances from relatives overseas.

So, returning to where we began. Your professors can lecture you on Engels, Marx, Hegel, Trotsky, and Lenin. That's their turf. I, on the other hand, offer you a reality check.

That is what I am compelled to do. Because I love you enough to give a damn!

-30-

Compassion!

It is written:

Feed a man a fish for he has hunger.
Teach a man to fish, he'll feed himself.
The first sates his hunger.
The second grants him dignity.
The first without the second creates dependency.
The second without the first invites failure.
So, which is compassionate?
Clearly both.

We hear differently

We hear a man. You hear a lie. I hear anguish. We hear a woman. You hear pain. I hear her bearing false witness against a man.

You hear Senator Blumenthal berating a man. I hear Senator Blumenthal claiming wartime service in Vietnam.

You hear Trump lying. I hear Trump using bombast and hyperbole to lay a foundation for negotiation.

You hear Hillary saying she was under combat fire upon arriving in Bosnia.

I hear and see the very videos of that arrival. No sniper fire. Nor did she miss the arrival greeting.

You hear Hillary reporting "an awful internet video" was to blame for the Benghazi attack.

I hear Hillary telling daughter Chelsea and the Egyptian Prime Minister that Benghazi was "a planned terrorist attack which had nothing to do with the film."

You hear Hillary denying classified information on her illegal personal server.

I read the law (U.S. Code) and find that Hillary violated the law just by having that off-site server, with or without classified information.

You hear Bill Clinton's "I did not have sexual relations with that woman." I hear that same former president expressing his being, "profoundly sorry for all I have done wrong in words and deeds," and "I never should have misled the country, the Congress, my friends and my family."

We could continue this list till we run out of paper.

Or, we could look at numbers. Try 62. That's the number of years Democrats controlled both houses of Congress in the 85 years from 1931 to 2016.

Here's another number. Try 73. That's the percentage of Detroit's eighth-grade students failing math proficiency. How about 44, 58, 51, and 48? Those are reading proficiency percentages for students in Detroit, Philadelphia, Baltimore, and Cleveland. And, yes, I can source this. Ask me.

More numbers. Here are 2016 Presidential election results for Chicago, Detroit, Baltimore, Philadelphia, and Cleveland: 83, 68, 84, 82, 75. Those are percentages favoring the Democrat candidate.

You see Democratic promises. I see Democrat failure.

You see Democrat victories. I see Democrat embezzlement. Promises not delivered.

I read Schweizer's *Clinton Cash.* You call it fabrication (if you read it at all). I read the footnotes and citations. I call it well-supported.

I read Attkisson's *Stonewalled.* You call it rubbish. I checked her biography and her sources. I call it well-supported investigative reporting.

I read Thomas Sowell and Walter Williams. I doubt if you do. These two black Ph.D. professor authors regularly illuminate the shortcomings of the Democrat Party.

So, yes. We hear differently. We read differently. But I am a trained critical listener and a skilled editor and evaluator who always checks sources: footnotes, works cited, and other references. You want to question mine? Just ask.

Now ask me why I distrust current Democrat leaders. Or, you could start at the top and read this letter again.

-30-

On Creation, a Synopsis

The psalmist wrote: *The heavens declare the glory of God.*

Today he might add: *All nature* declares the glory of God.

Why? Well, at the time Psalm 19 was written, humankind had not been aware of the Creator's instructions written upon genetic strands of DNA, nor had we been able to read the fingerprint-like identity of all matter by means of spectroscopy.

With these two advances of science -- the ability to read DNA and to identify every substance in the universe -- we humans can now see that God our Creator provides us a complete blueprint with which we can identify every bit of living organism and every bit of inanimate matter. In brief, all of the stuff of the universe -- be it human or beast, be it fish or fowl, be it reptile or insect, be it Giant Sequoia or diminutive clover, or be it rock or swirling cosmic gas. The Creator's catalog of pieces, parts, and designs. It's all there for us to see.

And this is probably why the Apostle Paul left us these thoughts:

> Romans 1:19 -- *For what may be known about God is plain to them, because God has made it plain to them.*
>
> And:
>
> Romans 1:20 -- *For since the creation of the world God's invisible qualities, His eternal power and divine nature, have been clearly seen, being understood from His workmanship, so that men are without excuse.*

And let us not overlook these final words: *so that men are without excuse.*

Without excuse for what? Well, that's made clear by the next verse: Fo*r although they knew God, they neither glorified Him as God nor gave thanks to Him, but they became futile in their thinking and darkened in their foolish hearts.*

Now consider this question: what do rocks, buffalos, ice cubes, and the Sun have in common?

Being subject to the laws of nature, each of these is continuously recycled. Continuously!

So in all of creation, nothing is wasted. Everything is and continues to be.

We calls this phenomena "cycles." The petrologic cycle (rock), biologic cycle (living organisms), hydrologic cycle (water), and astronomic cycle (stars, galaxies, and beyond).

And where we have cycles, we have recycles.

Of most recent attention is the astronomic cycle. Easy to visualize. Think supernova. We now perceive the life cycle of a star: birth, growth, maturity, aging, death.

We see fascinating Hubble photographs revealing post-supernova and pre-star formation. Swirling dust and gases destined to become new stars.

So "creation" offers DNA instructions, spectroscopy fingerprints, and discernible cycles. Everything identified. Everything in motion. Everything used not once, but countless times.

And we humans have the unmitigated gall, the audacity, the insolence, to consider ourselves the equal of our Creator! Woe the day we are recycled -- still arrogant, still unwilling to humble ourselves!

2019 On Erasing History

What is the best way to be certain we will repeat the errors of the past? Before we attempt to answer this, let's visit a coach and two books.

The best of football coaches – be they NFL or collegiate – are those who remember and teach the team's history. From the days of flickering black-and-white 16mm and 35mm motion picture cameras, right up today's HD videos, football coaches have used game videos.

An idle study? A pleasant pastime? Not at all. Our football coaches require their teams to review videos of past games. Our own team. Opponents. Identify errors. Notice weaknesses. Learn from errors. Improve performance. Prepare for the next game!

If you want to see a stark-raving mad coach, try telling him you just accidentally erased all video of last week's game! A seething outburst of anger may be the least of your worries.

Now let's consider two books. One portrays the 1789 French Revolution. This was just a few years following the end of our own American Revolutionary War: freedom and independence won from Britain, remember? This book – A Tale of Two Cities – reveals aristocrat tyranny as a cause of war and revolutionary excess, a result of war. Charles Dickens presents us with visions of revolutionary excess with gruesome scenes of bloody guillotines.

If you fail to see what Dickens' novel and our football coach have in common, let's take a look at a second book. This book features a wicked queen. She destroys righteous men who oppose her, even priests and prophets. Another character in this book is an evil idol-god who demands sacrifice of children. He uses fire to destroy children. The queen? Jezebel. The idol-god? Molech. The book? The Bible!

So, yes, even the Bible depicts flawed human behavior. Such examples serve to illustrate errors. Now return to the football coach. His team studies errors along with "best plays." This is also why we read A Tale of Two Cities and, for that matter, the Bible. The idea is to improve the present by studying the past.

In America it has taken us well over 200 years to correct some of our worst errors. Why would we want to erase artifacts of our history? Should we remember our past and correct errors, or forget and repeat our worst behaviors?

I argue in favor of remembering. Historic art - like San Francisco's George Washington mural, now set for destruction, is such an example. Statues, bridges, buildings, highways, schools - everywhere we see proposals to destroy. Books - yes, also the Bible - monuments, and art offer us an opportunity to learn from our mistakes and correct our behavior.

We should not hide our history. We should use our history. In all of its forms and genres, our history is the "how-to" book for self-improvement!

On Mueller Team First-String Attorneys

If a baker's dozen, frothing at the mouth, hungry as a pack of wolves, first-string Democrat attorneys, could not dig up indictable crimes to bag President Trump, are we being unreasonable if we believe it is now AG Barr's turn to seek truth?

Are we being unreasonable if we believe the deck was stacked against President Trump given 13 registered Democrats of the 17 Mueller investigation team members? Or, are we being unreasonable if we notice that 9 of the 17 Democrat Mueller team investigators donated substantial funds to Democrat candidates at election time?

I think not. Being reasonable may be "in the eye of the beholder" so to speak. But my sense of "reasonable" tends to respond to irrefutable facts, especially when those facts are offered by media clearly supporting "the other side."

It is one thing to hear the raw numbers but adding flesh to the bones does add a dimension of understanding. Hence this detailed list.

Below is the complete list of the special counsel team members, their donations and the party affiliation noted in their past or present voter registration records. **And, yes, 13 of the 17 team members are DEMOCRATS.** Admittedly, being Democrat is not a crime. But a 13 to 4 ratio does not come even close to a fair and balanced team. Notice also the "donations" data!

1) Brian M. Richardson, a former Supreme Court clerk and clerk for a judge serving on the U.S. Court of Appeals for the 2nd Circuit in New York City.

No donations.

Voter registration: No affiliation

2) Ryan Dickey, a lawyer on detail from the Justice Department Criminal Division's Computer Crime and Intellectual Property Section.

No donations.

Voter registration: DEMOCRAT.

3) Kyle Freeny, a lawyer from the Justice Department Criminal Division's Money Laundering and Asset Recovery Section

Freeny donated $250 to Barack Obama's presidential campaign in 2008, another $250 to Obama's reelection campaign in 2012 and $250 to Clinton's campaign in 2016.

Voter registration: DEMOCRAT.

4) Scott Meisler, an appellate lawyer from the Justice Department Criminal Division.

No donations.

Voter registration: No affiliation.

5) Zainab Ahmad, a lawyer from the U.S. Attorney's Office for the Eastern District of New York.

No donations

Voter registration: No affiliation.

6) **Greg Andres**, a former partner at Davis Polk, a former deputy assistant attorney general in the Justice Department Criminal Division and a former assistant U.S. attorney for the Eastern District of New York.

He donated $2,700 to the campaign of Sen. Kirsten Gillibrand (D-N.Y.) this year and $1,000 to the U.S. Senate campaign of David Hoffman (D) in 2009 when he ran unsuccessfully in Illinois.

Voter registration: DEMOCRAT

7) **Rush Atkinson**, a lawyer from the Justice Department Criminal Division Fraud Section.

He donated $200 to Clinton's campaign in 2016.

Voter registration: DEMOCRAT

8) **Michael Dreeben**, an appellate lawyer from the Office of the Solicitor General.

No donations.

Voter registration: DEMOCRAT.

9) **Andrew Goldstein**, a lawyer from the U.S. Attorney's Office for the Southern District of New York.

Goldstein donated $3,300 to Obama's campaigns in 2008 and 2012.

Voter registration: DEMOCRAT.

10) **Adam Jed**, an appellate lawyer from the Civil Division.

No donations.

Voter registration: DEMOCRAT.

11) Elizabeth Prelogar, an appellate lawyer on detail from the Office of the Solicitor General.

She donated $250 each to Clinton's campaign in 2016 and the Obama Victory Fund in 2012.

Voter registration: DEMOCRAT.

12) James Quarles, a former partner at Wilmer Hale and a former assistant special prosecutor for the Watergate Special Prosecution Force.

He donated more than $30,000 to various Democratic campaigns in 2016, including $2,700 to Clinton, although his giving spans two decades. Quarles also gave $2,500 in 2015 to Rep. Jason Chaffetz (R-Utah) and $250 to Sen. George Allen (R-Va.) in 2005.

Voter registration: DEMOCRAT

13) Jeannie Rhee, a former partner at Wilmer Hale who has served in the Office of Legal Counsel and as an assistant U.S. attorney in Washington.

Rhee donated a total of $5,400 to Clinton's campaign in 2015 and 2016, and a total of $4,800 to the Obama Victory Fund in 2008 and 2011. She also made smaller donations totaling $1,750 to the Democratic National Committee and to various Democrats running for Senate seats.

Voter registration: DEMOCRAT.

14) Brandon Van Grack, a lawyer on detail from the Justice Department's National Security Division.

He donated $286.77 to Obama's campaign in 2008.

Voter registration: DEMOCRAT.

15) Andrew Weissmann, a lawyer who headed the Criminal Division's Fraud Section. He has served as general counsel at the FBI and as an assistant U.S. attorney for the Eastern District of New York.

Weissmann donated $2,300 to the Obama Victory Fund in 2008, $2,000 to the DNC in 2006 and $2,300 to the Clinton campaign in 2007.

Voter registration: DEMOCRAT.

16) Aaron Zebley, a former partner at Wilmer Hale who has previously served with Mueller at the FBI and as an assistant U.S. attorney in the Eastern District of Virginia.

No donations.

Voter registration: No affiliation.

17) Aaron Zelinsky, a lawyer on detail from the U.S. attorney's office in the District of Maryland.

No donations.

Voter registration: DEMOCRAT.

By the way. I didn't make this up. I'm not a practitioner of fake news. I wrote the above introductory material. The rest is from a Washington Post article (not that I trust WAPO, but they did the research I would have done. They just came to different conclusions. Imagine that!

https://www.washingtonpost.com/news/post-politics/wp/2018/03/18/trump-said-muellers-team-has-13-hardened-democrats-here-are-the-facts/?utm_term=.e99b82b5fcef

--30—

On Losing the Electoral College

There are those among us who would abolish the electoral college. I am not one of those.

At this very moment, however, (April 2019) Democrats are setting about to strike down the electoral college. No, not setting about. They are already at it! And, in a fashion that surprises me not one whit, the Democrats are ignoring (violating?) our Constitution.

Why let a small thing like Article II, and for that matter Article V, get in the way? It's time for modernizing! Can't let old, dusty, ideas of ancient forefathers impede progress! Well, folks, it's time for us to stop sleeping at the wheel! The Mueller report is yesterday's snow! But Democrats would rather keep us focused on that! That way we'll not have time to deter their work. After all, dismantling the Constitution is best done out of the limelight.

If you think I am overstating the case, notice this: Democrats at "National Popular Vote" claim they now have secured 181 electoral votes, need only 89 more, and they claim the "bill" passed in 37 state legislative chambers.

Those are not my words. This is the latest update from the National Popular Vote website. What's that? You haven't heard of these folks? Go ahead. Track it down on the internet.

The Democrats are working like beavers building a dam. And the public doesn't appear (yet) to give a hoot. We had better catch up with the beavers!

Serious American voters know that what the National Popular Vote organization is doing is erroneous at best. The organization seems to have forgotten, or are studiously ignoring, the language of our Constitution. The very reason the signators of our Constitution established the electoral college was to prevent the popular vote from overriding the power and role of the States.

Why that? Well, what Democrats choose to ignore is what we citizens who recite the Pledge of Allegiance do not ignore: and to the Republic for which it stands.

If our founding fathers had desired to do so, this country could have been a popular democracy. But they did not so desire. That is why we are, in fact, a democratic republic. And that is what today's Democrats want to destroy. If they are successful, only citizens on the east and west coasts of our country need vote. The rest of the country might as well stay at home on election day.

And that, my friends, is why we have the electoral college. It is also why Democrats are busy today attempting to rid this country of that college.

To a heartbroken minister

Sir, I am compelled, perhaps inspired, to offer you what Jesus so often offers to each of us: that is, an opportunity. I fear you, and many within the Methodist fold, have fallen victim to our cultural dilution of words and ideas. Our Lord must be in agony, as He so often has been when we, His people, follow our own will even when we know it is in opposition to His.

Our culture, if not Satan himself, has perverted words like *inclusion*, *diversity*, and *progressive*. This, in a misguided quest for political correctness, and, I might add, the relentless herding of disparate groups into a single political fold.

I fear, Justin, that your church may be on the brink of offending the very Lord God that you seek to please. And I love you enough to pray that you might come to see inclusion not as we humans have come to define it, but rather as I believe God might envision it. He offers and seeks for us salvation. Is that not His idea of inclusion? Eternal and loving unity with those who reciprocate His love?

Allow me to explain. I'll start with *inclusion*. We should recall that when *many of his disciples turned back and no longer followed him,* Jesus did not restrain them. Dwell upon that for a moment.

The kind of inclusion the Bible repeatedly reveals to us is that which leads to union with God. And that inclusion always rests upon the choices we, His people, make.

A second category of a Biblical rendering of *inclusion* is that we must at all times focus upon the inclusion of all parts of His revealed, inspired, word. This, so that we do not exclude or ignore that which He wants us to know. Dwell also, please, upon that. We must leave cherry-picking to the harvesting of fruit.

Before concluding with the words *diversity* and *progressive*, permit me to offer these relevant thoughts. Your article states that some Christians are not as "concerned with things like divorce and extramarital sex" as they are with "gay clergy and marriages." This is where *inclusion* of the rest of the Bible comes in. Jesus adamantly condemns divorce and adultery (Mt 19). Yet, He condemned neither the woman at the well (Jn 4) nor the adulteress (Jn 8) to whom He said, "*Neither do I condemn thee: go, and sin no more.*) Jesus forgives. But forgiveness is not the same as condoning. And just as He does not condone divorce and adultery, neither does He condone homosexual behavior.

Justin, may I draw your attention to something I recently wrote to a certain Professor Copenhaver:

> Perhaps the most important thing Jesus says with respect to the topic of homosexuality is this: "*Do not think that I have come to abolish the Law or the Prophets; I have not come to abolish them but to fulfill them.*" He added, "*... not the smallest letter, not the least stroke of a pen, will by any means disappear from the Law until everything is accomplished.*"

Now what "Law" do we suppose Jesus is speaking about? Well, that would be the first five books of the Bible, the Torah. One of these is Leviticus within which chapters 18 and 20 make clear what Jesus and His Father think of "practicing" homosexuality. And for those who think Leviticus is only for Levite priests, look again. The Apostle Paul - whom Jesus not so gently recruited - offers the same advice in Romans 1.

True, Jesus does not utter the words "homosexual, homosexuality, or orientation." But He does clearly tell us that He neither abolishes nor changes the Law. And you as a Bible scholar surely know the "Law" he speaks of. And you know where to find this verse:

" '*Do not have sexual relations with a man as one does with a woman; that is detestable.*"

So, yes, Jesus does speak "of" homosexuality. This is not manipulation of the Bible, Professor. And, yes, those texts are relevant today, contrary to your statement otherwise. Do you believe Jesus errs when he says *"... not the smallest letter, not the least stroke of a pen, will by any means disappear from the Law until everything is accomplished"* ? Do you believe everything has been accomplished?

Finally, my article did not say Jesus abhors the homosexual person, or, for that matter, the adulterous person. You and I both know what He does abhor: actions which preclude our eternal union with Him. He wants us. He wants us to want

> Him. We must all want Him enough to sacrifice that which He abhors. For homosexuals that sacrifice is an act of love He will not forget.

So, Justin, I'll now return to the words *diversity,* and *progressive.* In recent years these two words have become corrupted. They are buzzwords, the slogans, the planks of a political party which is relentlessly engaging in the destruction of Christian thought and practice. This party does so when it condones and promotes behaviors that are clearly in opposition to what my Bible and yours state so clearly.

So, you should thank your African Methodist delegates. They may be offering your final opportunity. They may be another of God's messengers to whom He said, "*I raised you up for this very purpose, that I might display My power in you.*"

Yes, God wants inclusion and diversity. He wants all of His people to willfully respond, to reciprocate His love, to follow Jesus, to join the Father. Yet, we must remember:

> When *many of his disciples turned back and no longer followed him,* Jesus did not restrain them.

Justin, this letter is my prayer that you and all members of churches now facing division and destruction might not find the quest for *inclusion* resulting rather in self-selected *exclusion.*

I am Frank Tilton, a septuagenarian but neither priest nor minister. Just a neighbor and fellow Christian.

(Added note: This letter exceeds the acceptable length for the Winchester Star. I may offer an edited version roughly half this length, without disclosing your name. But I do share letters such as these with members of my local Bible study and similar groups. We discuss. We pray. We continue to read the Bible.)

--30--

2019 March16 Sermon
How to Pray for our Foe

I am indebted to you, Fr. John Paul, for your most beneficial March 16, 2019, sermon. You have led me out of a quandary.

I have long sought the "how," as in "how to *love one's enemy*, and how to *be perfect as God is perfect*?"

Those, until today, have seemed to me to be unachievable goals. For how can I love someone – as in your cited New Zealand example – who has viciously slaughtered dozens of innocent victims while they were worshiping God? And how can any human fulfill "*Be you therefore perfect, as also your heavenly Father is perfect"?*

But your sermon offered me the key to unlocking this dilemma. You have opened my mind to a greater understanding of the word "grace."

You told me that grace is God's gift of the Holy Spirit. *His* Holy Spirit. And, yes, I had seen this elsewhere in Scripture. More than a few examples.

And I have often explored the nature of love, and other gifts, which are, and can be, complete only with reciprocity.

ut you added several layers of enlightenment when you said that being perfect as the Father is perfect is possible *only with grace.* That grace, the gift of the Holy Spirit, is essential: it is that ingredient which makes possible reciprocity. Without the gift, there is nothing to reciprocate. Without reciprocity the gift is not, cannot be, complete.

For me, the "key" was how you clarified that God's gift (of the Holy Spirit) is:

*in us (within us)

*without us (meaning both external to us and without our effort or cooperation)

*with us (with, as together, and with, by means of our cooperation)

*through us (by means of *our* visible actions as purveyors of God's grace)

And this, Fr. Paul, led me to understand, finally, how to love one's enemy. We must love him by offering prayer for him. We must pray that he will repent, that he will accept and reciprocate God's gift of the Holy Spirit, that he will seek and accept the gift of salvation.

In this way, we do not condone or excuse his reprehensible actions. Rather, we pray that he might, as we must, choose to act upon God's precious gift of grace that we *might be perfect as the Father is perfect.*

So, thank you. And with, and by God's grace, may you continue the reciprocity of love.

On Why God Allows Evil

I've been seeking to learn why it is God, our Creator, allows so much evil. It is a perplexing question.

I suppose I should start with full disclosure. I'm not a pastor, minister, or priest. Nor am I a theologian. Actually, I'm just one of you! You and I, those who are curious. Being curious is probably a good thing even at my age -- beyond-seven-decades. I believe there is God. Also that He created all that is. With that as a foundation, let's get back to evil.

As long as there have been two or more humans on this planet, there has been evil. Let's face it. At the outset, Adam and Eve were given but one rule. It seems they took very little time breaking that one rule. Some time later they gave birth to two sons. One of those sons murdered the other.

So evil has clearly always been an ingredient of human behavior. Seems odd, doesn't it? Countless humans over the centuries have asked, "How could a God who created us and who loves us saddle us with so much evil?"
We look about and observe a plethora of evil human behavior. As evidence, we see greed, pride, lies, deception, theft, corruption, and lewd conduct. Human history seethes with examples. So does our present day. Examples abound!

But getting back to the perplexing question. Why so much evil? In our effort to unravel that 'why so much evil' question, we will need to examine three topics: the nature of God, the ingredients of love, and God's gift of free will. All of this will clearly be illustrated within an ancient narrative story.

We could begin with that story. But first, a quick review of a couple of things we understand to be true about God. He created us. He loves us. He wants us to be with Him in eternity. There is more, of course. But one characteristic in particular is relevant to our discussion here: He is omniscient. Knowing all makes perfect sense once we've established that He created all.

But, given that He knows all, doesn't that mean that He knows we humans will do evil things? And if He knows the evil we will do, why does He not prevent us from doing so? This is a good time to turn to the story. I particularly like this narrative because it explains and clarifies so much. Let's meet Joseph.

This Joseph is not the spouse of Mary who gave birth to Jesus. No, we must go all the way back to the book of Genesis to meet this Joseph. This Joseph is the son of Jacob, who was the son of Isaac. That makes this Joseph the grandson of Abraham.

The story is an early Biblical example of human evil. Joseph's brothers were jealous and hated him. So they sold Joseph, Jacob's favored son, to traders headed for Egypt. Eventually, Joseph was sold to an officer of the Pharaoh.

Evil behavior! And this while God, knowing all, was looking on. This seems contrary to what we humans think we know about God. Much of our Sunday-school teaching tends to focus on another characteristic about "Our Father who art in Heaven." That characteristic is love. So let's focus now on love.

Over the years – my years, that is -- I have given no small amount of thought to the topic of love. In brief, what I came up with is this. First, love is a gift. It's God's gift to us. But it also is our gift to other humans.

Now, the most essential characteristic of love – whether that from God or that from humans – is that it is incomplete, it cannot and will not survive, without being returned. That "return loop" is called reciprocity.

Think of an elongated oval. Imagine this egg-shaped figure – also called elliptical – having embedded arrows. One arrow is outbound love destined for a recipient. Once it reaches its target, the recipient has choices. Receive or reject. Retain or return. If we decide to receive and return love, the arrow now travels along that same oval back to the source of the gift. That's reciprocity.

Soon we'll return to our story of Joseph whose life as a servant of the Pharaoh has placed the young lad in a position of great responsibility. Joseph has become the Pharaoh's highest officer with command of both the royal household and the entire country of Egypt. But first let's get back for now to love and that oval of reciprocity.

Once the gift of love has been sent, received, and returned, we can see that the process is complete. Had the gift been rejected, or even received but simply retained like a box on a closet shelf, the cycle is incomplete. Without reciprocity, then, love withers and dies like a plant without water.

But now we come to the most important point. And it is this point which explains why it is God allows evil to exist.

We have said that once the gift of love reaches its target, the recipient has choices. Receive or reject. Retain or return. Choices! We call these choices free will.

When God created humans, He gave them - and each of us - free will. Some theologians are still looking for those words in the Bible. But what they should be looking for is not the word. Rather, free will is found in Genesis as action.

Our most distant parents, remember, were given that one rule in the Garden of Eden. They were not to eat the fruit of one particular tree. But they did so. They chose to eat that fruit. That "choice" was possible only because they had free will.

And why were they, and we, given that "choice" to do or not do? Now we are approaching the answer to our dilemma: the why of evil. The answer is found within our search for the nature of love. Choices.

It is free will that allows us to *receive* or *reject, retain* or *return.* And our Creator understood the risk. He gave us free will. But He recognized we might choose *reject* and *retain* rather than *receive* and *return.* Why did He take that risk?

We must think of free will in binary terms. It is either free or not free. It cannot be both. Our Lord knew that. So now, let's return to thinking about the nature of love.

The only way God's love for His humans can be complete is if we choose to accept, receive, and return that love. And the only way that can happen is for us to have the freedom to choose. Hence, free will.

Human history is chock full of examples of human free will gone awry!

Now we'll examine one more crucially important distinction. Earlier we noted that God is omniscient. But *knowing* is not the same as *causing*. It is also not the same as *allowing*. Actually, I'm convinced that God's knowing often causes Him no small amount of agony. After all, which of us would enjoy knowing ahead of time and with absolute certainty that something horribly tragic is about to happen?

Imagine watching your son, just beyond the age of toddler. He's reaching for a pot of boiling water on the stove. You know what is about to happen. In my book *Eternity*, I wrote:

"And you watch. But you do not move. Every muscle and nerve in your body twitches then knots itself into a searing, painful mass of energy. Still you don't interfere because you gave your son free will. And what seconds ago was Jeremy's inquisitive little face is now .... Your knowledge has just turned to agony. Gut-wrenching, nauseating agony."

So, returning to our story of Joseph - his brothers do evil, sell him as slave. All the while our Lord God knew in advance what was to happen. He knew also that He would not intervene in the action thus negating free will.

So, what did He do instead? He used their evil deed to the ultimate benefit of others. How did this play out?

Many years after their evil deed, Joseph's brothers find themselves standing before the Pharaoh's mightiest officer. Notice what follows:

"I am Joseph, your brother," he said, "the one you sold into Egypt! And now, do not be distressed or angry with yourselves that you sold me into this place, because *it was to save lives that God sent me before you.* For the famine has covered the land these two years, and there will be five more years without plowing or harvesting. *God sent me before you to preserve you as a remnant on the earth and to save your lives by a great deliverance. Therefore, it was not you who sent me here, but God,* who has made me a father to Pharaoh—lord of all his household and ruler over all the land of Egypt." (Genesis 45)

And near the end of the story, following the death of Jacob (also called Israel), the brothers fear Joseph will seek revenge for their misdeed. But Joseph quells their fear:

"As for you, what you intended against me for evil, God intended for good, in order to accomplish a day like this—to preserve the lives of many people." (Genesis 50)
And now we can return to the perplexing question which launched this venture.

We have learned that God loves us. But we have also learned that His love can reach fruition, become complete, only if we choose to receive it, accept it, and return it. We also discovered that such a choice is an available option to all humans only because of yet another of God's gifts. Free will.

Finally, when we abuse free will with our misdeeds, God may use our evil to achieve His own goal. His goal? The greater good - the salvation of all *humans who choose to receive and return* His gift of love.

We must not conclude this reflection on the why of evil, however, without this final clarification. It is important for us to recognize the distinction between the words *so that* and the word *and.* Our Creator, our Lord, does not allow evil *so that* He might use it. *So that* implies purpose. This could lead us to believe that He wants us to engage in evil. He clearly does not wish us to do evil. Rather, He allows freedom of choice, *and* He may use our flawed choices and their consequences to bring about a greater good. Let us recognize: *so that* implies intent while *and* does not do so.

And that, dear readers, is my answer to this perplexing question.

Tilton Books 2017

A Lake Frederick couple, Frank and Josefine Tilton, will be offering a unique art event at the community's Shenandoah Club with its Region's 117 restaurant this June. Josie is an artist specializing in abstracts, and both are authors. The event will feature a display of Josie's art and a "signing day" for her book and for five of Frank's books. (Date to be announced but probably June 7, the first "happy hour" of the month).

-

The couple have been Lake Frederick residents since May, 2010, and have been active pursuing their art and writing interests. Josie teaches and hosts a twice monthly Artistes de Couleur group in the Shenandoah Club. Frank facilitates and hosts a weekly men's Bible study in their Turnstone Lane home.

The "artist-author" event will be open to both the Lake Frederick community and to the public. Those who attend will be treated to a glass of wine for each "signed" book they purchase, although it is not necessary to buy either a book or art to join in the event.

The six books - listed below - represent many weeks, months, and years of the couple's lives. Married just 53 years, the two have lived in Germany and the United States while pursuing careers and raising a family. Frank was a career U.S. Air Force officer. That 24-year stint was followed by 19 years as a middle school teacher of English and German. Josie was a career Federal civil servant who began with a new language and culture at the age of twenty and culminated her 30-year career as a Senior International Trade Specialist for the U.S. Commerce Department.

Their books range from Josie's autobiography (her life began behind the Iron Curtain) to a mélange of genres by Frank - a Cold War spy novel, a realistic science fiction novel, a Bible-based grammar textbook for middle school students, a "how to" book for parents of middle school students, and an inspirational inquiry into the nature of eternity and creation.
These two Lake Frederick residents came to Virginia from Indiana.

Their books are:

"Tumbleweed" - by Josefine Tilton
"Eternity" - by Frank Tilton
"Grappling with God and Grammar" - by Frank Tilton
"How to Cope with those Middle School Years" - by Frank Tilton
"The Qanaq Conundrum" - by Frank Tilton
"What? No Babies?" - by Frank Tilton

"Tumbleweed" - by Josefine Tilton records events I experienced as a young girl in Germany living first under the Communist regime, then within the "economic miracle" of West Germany, and finally my years as an immigrant and military spouse in the United States. This is my story about people who live under extreme circumstances, people who conquer the fear of taking risks. The story is about being a refugee from East Germany trying to fit in and be accepted by fellow Germans on the other side of the iron curtain. The story is about an immigrant who despite a lack of English language skills learns the language then competes in the workplace and overcomes obstacles to career advancement in the world's most wonderful country. My story is about a young woman who encounters a life-threatening disease and how she became a survivor.

....

"Eternity" - by Frank Tilton is a scholarly yet lighthearted look at life's biggest question. It examines the nature of eternity together with its nearly inseparable partner, creation, in a narrative blend of light-hearted and "fire-up-the neurons" reading. It takes a refreshing, up-to-date look at a topic of increasing interest to all who have been bludgeoned by the atrocities of modern life. Eternity - a scholarly yet lighthearted look at life's biggest question -- is a book for all who seek, who question, who enjoy chasing curiosity to the ends of, well, wherever it ends. Starting with a single but explosive Bible quotation, Jer 1: 4-5, (*Before I formed you in the womb I knew you*"), the author takes readers on an inquisitive, rational, and sometimes jocular journey into the mystery of how it is for humans that there is no present, and how it is for God there is no past or future. We investigate the real reason for our creation and then grapple with the creation issue itself. En route we explore knowing, loving, and thinking.

....

"Grappling with God and Grammar" - by Frank Tilton is a Scripture-based English grammar textbook for Christian high school or middle school. It is equally suitable for Catholic and non-Catholic private schools and for the growing Christian home school market. This textbook uses the Bible itself to teach English grammar. Each page contains Scripture, discussion of the daily reading, the grammar lesson of the day, a vocabulary nugget, a bonus question, and the daily student assignment.

....

"How to Cope with those Middle School Years" - by Frank Tilton offers parents of soon-to-be middle school students a means of coping with the transition from the pleasantries of elementary school to the mind-morphing realities of middle school. In a "how to cope" collection of survival tips, retired middle school teacher Frank Tilton offers parents knowledge nuggets he has mined in his own years of parenting and middle school teaching. Parents, especially those of current fifth grade students, soon will be asking, "Is there a light at the end of the tunnel?" In How to Cope with those Middle School Years they will discover both the short and the long answers to that question. But first those parents must find ways to keep up with, get ahead of, and outwit their own Susies, Sams, Sarahs, or Seths. To do this, parents will need to know what to expect and what to do before, during, and after middle school. And they need to know these things before Susie knows them.

....

"The Qanaq Conundrum: The Cold War's Coldest Commander" - by Frank Tilton is a Cold War Spy thriller. An Air Force captain arrives for assignment at Thule Air Base, Greenland. He soon discovers the body of a fellow officer floating in a nearby fjord. As winter darkens the arctic, Captain Ross burrows ever deeper into the mystery of the officer's death. Thule's own "Cold War" claims victim after victim as officers and non-coms are snared into traps leading to their own destruction. The story takes us from the Cold War's northernmost outpost to the streets of Berlin, Germany, before revealing the ugliest of outcomes.

....

"What? No Babies?" - by Frank Tilton is a realistic science fiction inquiry into a world without babies. An Air Force doctor notices babies are no longer being conceived.

Elsewhere, a lieutenant in the Air Force's NORAD command center pursues his curiosity about a comet. Both are ridiculed. Yet both are right to be concerned. Kinderman's Comet had partially vaporized as it passed through perihelion. Earth passed through the comet's tail and became contaminated by an undetected virus. The story follows Doctor Dan Holland who learned how "Copernicus must have felt ..." as he tries to convince contentious Washington that he knows the cause of the world-wide zero conception rate. Washington and the rest of the world begin to awaken to the reality of the virus' scourge. Yet few are willing to listen to this Air Force physician who argues, "We're trying to find a way to keep human beings on the planet. There's no time now for politics." Nation accuses nation. Terrorists seek revenge. Kidnappers supply children to a hungry market. Drugs, alcohol, and human folly further reduce a rapidly declining population. A world without children emerges. School playgrounds rust. America comes to look like Pompeii without the ashes. (This is also available in a German language edition under the title "Kindermann's Komet.")

-30-

Part Two
On my Air Force Career

My USAF Years:

1961, June: The Train

At the Armed Forces processing center in Los Angeles, I passed a physical exam and then boarded a train bound for San Antonio, Texas. The train was stuffed with guys headed for basic training. All through the night I heard rhythmic clicks and clacks as the train snaked its way through California and Arizona deserts. I lay on a narrow upper bunk and watched a full moon dart in and out of view behind rock-strewn mountains and shadowy saguaro, the cactus with arms upraised as if in welcome, or surprise.

I was disinclined to strike up much of a conversation with anyone for I had just left behind a girl who, at that time, I thought was the love of my life. But what does a seventeen-year-old know about either of those weighty topics – love, life?

Night became day, and Arizona became New Mexico as the train rumbled along. Most of the fellows were playing cards, smoking, swilling down beer, and drowning one another out with loud tales of football exploits, cars, girls, and what they already knew about the Air Force. I did not consider myself expert on any of those topics, so I pretty much kept to myself. My two older brothers had gone to sea with the Navy, but I had opted for the Air Force in large part owing to the influence of my "Uncle Mac." He was a career Air Force non-com, at the time of my train trip to basic training, a master sergeant. My visits with him at March Air Force Base in Riverside had given me a taste of Air Force life. Mac was calm and gentle and always seemed to know far more than he said. His serenity and sagacity was juxtaposed by the angry roar of eight jet engines as B-52 bombers lumbered down the runway then launched themselves into the air. These were among my thoughts as the train took me farther away from home than I had ever before been.

It was late at night when our train came to a shuddering halt in San Antonio. The bravado boys had quieted down, glowing tips of cigarettes being the chief sign they were still awake. We didn't arrive unexpected. A small fleet of dusty blue buses and shouting, uniformed airmen – some non-coms -- awaited us. We were sworn at, cussed at, and herded into the buses before a single one of us could make the slightest misstep or head off in the wrong direction.

1961, July-Oct. Basic Training.

We were called "rainbows." Derisive shouts flew at us from all directions that first day. "Rainbows" was the least offensive term we'd hear for several days. It simply categorized us as beginners, novices, new kids on the block because we were wearing colorful "civvies." Uniform issue didn't take place until day three. I think our "T.I's" had been told to wait a day or two to see who among us would collapse and be sent home before they issued us uniforms. Speaking of "T.I's" - the Air Force term for drill instructor - ours were Sergeants Pagliara and Hall. Fifty-two years (as of this writing) after basic training I still remember those names. That should tell you something about basic training.

Tech Sergeant Pagliara was thin. No, make that spare and wiry like a cowhand. He was light of hair and wore a uniform cap, grunge- green, which looked as though it had been laundered, starched, and stretched over a coffee-can to dry. He was the tough one. Hall, a staff sergeant, was more genial, both in appearance and in demeanor. He was also the first black man I had ever seen up close and personal. I was mesmerized by his appearance. As with Pagliara's, Hall's uniform was starched, creased, and inspection ready. Hall was stout, about the same height as Pagliara, but less athletic looking. I couldn't take my eyes off him. I was fascinated by his hands, black on the finger-nail side, but light, almost pink on the palm side. I found myself wondering whether his feet were similarly of dual colors.

His tongue was so pink, it looked like bubble-gum. Altogether he was a pleasant-looking fellow. But the Texas sun soon brought beads of sweat to his entire face, and in no time at all the back of his shirt sported a football size dark blotch of perspiration. Pagliara, on the other hand, seemed, always, to be dry as a weathered cedar plank.

There are a good many things one never forgets about basic training. For me, one that tops the list is what happened that first morning. We had finally bunked down after a three-day train ride, a blurry and flurry of hustle and bustle, more swearing and yelling than I had ever in my then young life heard, and strangers everywhere. We tumbled wearily onto wafer-thin mattresses supported by springs stretched between the frames of steel-framed bunk beds. Sleep was as instant as a light switch. But .... It was at oh-five-hundred (5 a.m.) that the loudest, shrillest, chromed steel whistle known to mankind blasted us upright and out of our bunks. My stomach felt like I had just swallowed, in a single gulp, five pounds of frozen cottage cheese. A new day had started. And every day for the next several weeks would begin in exactly the same way, with both the whistle and the frozen cottage cheese.

We tumbled out of bunks all scitter and scatter. Some guys were wearing boxer shorts, others briefs. Wrinkled t-shirts, crumpled tank-tops, or the "bare look" were the motif of the day – if, in fact, it was "day." Pagliara sped down the middle of the motley crew sputtering epithets the likes of which none of us had ever heard. He zeroed in not on those in greatest disarray but on one hapless toad who had slept in his clothes. Loosely, and somewhat civilly translated what the raging "T.I." shouted was, "You illegitimate son of an itinerant ignoramus, you shame the very mother who brought you into this world." The toad was on the deck doing pushups before any of us could blink. Then he was further berated for the non-military manner in which was performing the pushups. Something to do with the way worms have sexual relations.

Pagliara's next target was the chump caught laughing. The rest of us went silent while our "T.I." compared the now pale source of the laughter with the "south end of a northbound hyena." Though Pagliara's eyes remained fixed on the toad, "we" were instructed that we would laugh when ordered to do so, speak when ordered to do so, cough when ordered to do so, and crap when ordered to do so. And with that, the whole lot of us were doing pushups while Pagliara shouted complaints to all the gods of Olympus that he, an honorable "Tech Sergeant," had been saddled with the sorriest collection of girl scouts known to man.

The next thing we knew we were outside on pavement and being harangued into some sort of military formation. All the stars of the Milky Way were puncturing holes into an otherwise black sky. Not the slightest hint of daylight anywhere. Day one of Air Force basic training had begun. And we were a sleepy, rag-tag bunch of rainbows with the shrill of that steel whistle still ringing in our ears.

This would be a good place to describe who "we" were. The train I had arrived on was but one of several such trains that day. So "we" were kids from all around the country. Most of us were eighteen or nineteen. One or two may have been twenty. I was seventeen. We were tall, short, thin, and stout. The majority of us had just graduated from high school and had just "cut mom's apron strings." In those years kids typically left the "nest" at the age of eighteen to begin jobs, college, or the military. "We" had all opted for the Air Force. So here we were, out under a Texas sky so early even birds and rattlesnakes were still sleeping. There was not a single airplane anywhere to be seen. And we were "rainbows." Tech Sergeant Pagliara shouted us into a semblance of a military formation and informed us "we" were henceforth to be known as "Flight 919." This was followed by a piercing, "Fliiiiiight, tench hut!" The list of identifiers we were never to forget began to grow. We were flight nine-nineteen, 3120th Training Squadron, commanded by Major William Huxworthy, and our barracks was Building 748, Lackland Air Force Base, Texas.

Basic training is many things, and only one of these is "training." To bring about the conversion of young men from rainbows to "airmen," our "T.I's" had to break us down before they could build us up. The first thing to go was hair. If there is a Guinness Book of Records entry for speedy haircuts, surely this tops the list. Thirty-six guys file in with windblown "duck tails" and greasy globs of sweaty hair, pay 35-cents, mount a barber's chair, and file out with heads looking like boiled eggs. All in less than three minutes. Well, okay, the fact that there were ten barbers factors into the equation. The end result was that there was a large enough pile of hair on the floor to stuff a mattress for Paul Bunyan, and "Flight 919" was back outside looking, and feeling, rather sheepish.

Right away we were issued our first uniform item - the pith helmet a.k.a. safari helmet. Now we looked like a bedraggled band of would-be hunters ready to track wildebeest in the Serengeti. The pith helmet, however, was a welcome if somewhat unexpected gift. The blazing Texas sun would have cooked our newly shorn noggins lobster-red in mere minutes. Those pith helmets would be our constant companions for the next several weeks.

Flight 919 walked - make that "marched" - everywhere we went. We would "fall out" (from within a building) and "fall in" once outside. We would "dress right" to straighten our lines, and "right face" to get our four columns aiming a single direction. Those who failed to properly distinguish between "right" and "left" would promptly perform push-ups and then carry - with right arm extended pencil-straight - a grapefruit-sized stone. And then, to remind us that we were a "flight" rather than an assemblage of individuals, Pagliara would order all of us down for "50" when one of us "trucked-up." Flight 919 did lots of pushups. And "trucked-up," of course, is a euphemism for what Pagliara actually said. That four-letter word for sexual intercourse (rhyming with "truck") flavored Tech Sergeant Pagliara's utterances, orders, commands, and general vocabulary with the frequency of a hummingbird flapping his wings. I began to wonder, with all that "trucking" going on, how it was that Flight 919 didn't become pregnant. Or at least catch gonorrhea. But there was little time for humor, and clearly no future in being a wise ass. Basic training, I had already decided, was a good place to practice the camouflage techniques of a chameleon. Blend, baby, blend. Blend and survive.

So, Flight 919 marched everywhere it went. We marched to a supply building where we sidestepped briskly down a line while airmen – their single striped sleeves attesting to the fact that their careers were not much riper than ours – plunked items down upon a three-foot-wide shelf in front of us. The first item was a dark blue duffle bag. By the time I had sidestepped to the far end of this shelf, I had been "issued" some $300 worth of clothing. That was more, by far, than the entire wardrobe I had left behind at home in California. Into that duffle bag I had stuffed combat boots, black leather shoes, black socks, shirts, trousers, undershorts, t-shirts, hats, belts, and even a blue wool overcoat larger, longer, and heavier than any item of clothing I had ever seen. The duffle bag seemed to weigh 300 pounds – I calculated a buck a pound. In fact, it was closer to 100 but more likely didn't come in at much over 75 pounds. Off we marched, sort of. Flight 919 on its return journey to Building 748. We must have looked like a herd of centipedes carrying barrels of molasses on our backs. It was the first time – the only time – Pagliara didn't send us to the gravel for pushups as our marching was anything but military precision. He seemed intent only on getting us back inside the barracks before any of his fellow "T.I's" caught sight of us. Of course, the entire way back to the barracks we were berated for being a gaggle of "trucking" girl scouts!

The next day's "training" left little time for marching. We started "obstacle" training by climbing 30-foot ropes up the face of a cliff. The cliff was natural, probably sandstone. At the top were the "T.I's" – our two and half a dozen others. They were "urging" us to get up and over that cliff. I could see that the ropes were attached to permanently mounted log fixtures so it looked safe enough. In fact, I thought it would the first "fun" thing we had yet attempted. We trainees were lined up each in our own squad. The whistles blew and one-by-one we ran toward the cliff, grabbed the rope and hoisted ourselves up the face of that cliff. I was immediately behind a guy who looked like he'd been on a high school football squad. He was sturdy looking. Squared and rugged. But as he started up the rope he struggled mightily. It didn't look to me as if he'd done this sort of thing before. And his weight was a detriment. Great for the football team, especially if he had been a lineman. But slowly he inched his way up while Pagliara berated him with foul invectives at top volume. The guy made it within a foot of the top. Then he began to cry! That didn't go over well with Pagliara. I began to wonder of the T.I.s at the top had placed bets. They were certainly more than a little energetic about getting their squads to the top in short order. So the sturdy looking guy in front of me was wailing like a baby with its fingers caught in a car door. Pagliara yelled out, "Go back down, you turd! Start over!" And the guy followed the order, but without thinking. He released the rope with both hands. Down he went like a sack of potatoes. He hit the ground directly in front of me. Broke both legs. More wailing. The medics hauled him off on a stretcher. And now it was my turn to ascend the cliff. So off I went, scared as hell. I went up faster than a monkey. Talk about adrenalin! By the way. The sturdy-looking football lineman didn't finish basic training. I did not see him again. He missed what I thought to be the best part of basic training. Over the next several days we climbed and roped over water obstacles, climbed all sorts of barricades, and fired a 30-calibre rifle on the firing range. I scored well in all of those events. And soon enough basic training was over. I was headed off to the "real" world.

Frank-Cold War

Most of my Air Force career was dedicated to what history now calls the Cold War. Within the first two years of my Air Force life, I found myself involved in three major Cold War events. The first of these was the 1961 Berlin Crisis.

Cold War, Berlin Crisis of 1961:

This is best remembered today as the time when Russian troops partitioned Berlin while East Germany constructed the (concrete portions) of the Berlin Wall. Little did I know at the time that this event would change my life forever. What I did know during the final days of my Air Force basic training was that tensions were high in Berlin and that I and my fellow trainees were swept quickly into phase two of our training because of these tensions. Many of us packed our duffel bags (all of our earthly belongings) and boarded buses for Keesler Air Force Base, Mississippi. Rumors were rampant that we'd all be shipped off to Germany. But first we had to complete our training at Keesler. We became "Morse intercept operators." That is, we learned to "listen" to the Morse Code and type coded messages at a speed of thirty-six character groups per minute. I actually did very well at this. And, yes, I was shipped off to Germany. But once I arrived at Rhein Main Air Base, I joined 30 or 40 others in a large room with only a few chairs and a chalkboard. A sergeant randomly took twenty of our names and wrote them on the chalkboard. Mine was last on the list. "You twenty are going to

Darmstadt," he shouted. I was disappointed because I and two of my friends had wanted to go to Italy. Then, the sergeant returned to the chalkboard and re-counted. Oops. There were 21 names on his list. He erased the last name. I and my two friends went to Italy! And, no, we didn't have computers in those days.

Cold War, Italy assignment, 1962:

When I arrived in Italy the Cold War - for me - went from concept to reality. Our "operations" building was without windows, partially underground, and surrounded by security guards and barbed-wire. As you've probably guessed from my training at Keesler, my job was to listen to Morse Code messages. Now, as long as mankind on this planet has engaged in warfare (all of human history) it has been necessary to know as much as possible about the enemy. How many are they? What are their weapons? Where are they located? That sort of thing. That'll give you some idea of why I was listening to Morse Code messages. We listened. We copied. We translated. We sent reports. And when we weren't working, we went to the beach. It was southern Italy, after all. After several months, though, I developed a medical problem, went to a hospital in North Africa, lost my security clearance, and was reassigned to Germany.

Cold War, Cuban Missile Crisis, October 14-28, 1962

I had been at Hahn Air Base, Germany, only a few days when the Cold War began to look a bit more toasty than frigid. The Russians decided to position nuclear missiles in Cuba, we Americans decided that such was not acceptable.

After all, those missiles were capable of reaching Washington, D.C. Hahn was both a tactical and an air defense fighter base, so when the Cuban Missile Crisis went hot, Hahn went to DEFCON 3. For me, that meant flight line perimeter defense. Being an enlisted fellow who didn't pilot aircraft (the Air Force was smart enough to keep me as far from a cockpit as possible), my duty was guarding a strip of concrete which for some 2-1/2 miles nestled up to the darkest of German forests just minutes by air from our Russian adversaries in East Germany. So there I was. Armed with a .30-cal rifle - but lacking any ammunition - patrolling my segment of the airfield. Twelve-hour shifts. Cold. But there was one highlight. I got to meet a shepherd. Most foul-smelling human being on the planet! He was there because he had a contract with the base to graze his sheep along the airfield. That was how we kept the grass trimmed, I learned. And that was how the shepherd kept his sheep fed. I tried chatting with the fellow. He spoke no German. Nor did I at that point. So there wasn't much conversation. The Cuban Missile Crisis ended after about two weeks. President Kennedy had delivered a nation-wide televised address announcing the discovery of the missiles and conveying this message to Russia's Nikita Khrushchev:

It shall be the policy of this nation to regard any nuclear missile launched from Cuba against any nation in the Western Hemisphere as an attack by the Soviet Union on the United States, requiring a full retaliatory response upon the Soviet Union.

That warning, together with some 511 tactical fighters (ours) and multiple squadrons of B-52 bombers on 24-hour airborne alert (ours), not to mention deployed Army divisions (ours), Naval blockades (ours), and, oh yes, me guarding the Hahn Air Base flight line, well, Khrushchev reconsidered the whole deal. For my part, I was glad he did so. Here's why:

The resulting war might have led to the deaths of 100 million Americans and over 100 million Russians. (*Graham Tillett Allison, Jr. American political scientist and professor at the John F. Kennedy School of Government, Harvard University.*)

As time would go by, and as I progressed from the enlisted ranks to a commissioned officer, I would have much more to do with the Cold War. Nothing comparable to what my brother Dan was up against with his combat missions in the Vietnam War. But dicey enough at times. More about those assignments later. And, oh, getting back to that Berlin Wall. That event that "would change my life forever" - well, it did. That was how I met Josefine Lohse. Most of you know her better as Josie Tilton. Her story ... well, you can read that in her book, Tumbleweed.

Cold War, 1963, the Kennedy Assassination

My years at Hahn Air Base were momentous and memorable. A period of growth for me. No, I remained about 5'10" and held close to 145 pounds. But the "teen" years tended to fade rather quickly. The tempo and the temperature of the Cold War added a certain reality check to everything I was doing. Hahn was home base to two tactical fighter squadrons flying F-100 Super Sabres (like those pictured above) and one air defense squadron flying F-102 Delta Daggers.

And, no, I have never made a claim to have been a pilot, though folks often ask me such. My standard response to that inquiry is: “Oh, hell no! The Air Force is a lot smarter than that! I’m the last guy on the planet the Air Force would want in a cockpit!” I usually follow that exclamation with my “two switches” in the kitchen story. I’m the guy with a sleepy face who approaches the kitchen sink at about oh-dark-thirty in the morning. There are two switches. One for the lights. One for the garbage disposal. You got it! I startle the tarnation out of myself by hitting the garbage disposal switch! Aaaarrrgh! And then I say to myself, “And that, you turkey, is precisely why you are not and never will be a pilot!”

But okay, I was not a pilot. Truth be told, about 97% of Air Force people are not and were not ever pilots. The Air Force has always needed far more mechanics, fire fighters, weapons loaders, and pencil-pushers than it needed pilots. And I was one of those. Pencil-pushers, that is. At the time of the Cuban Missile Crisis, I was an orderly room clerk for the 496th Fighter Interceptor Squadron. I remember sitting in an office with Airman Timothy Goombi, an Apache Indian. He and I were pounding typewriters completing DD forms 398 so that squadron members could obtain their security clearances. That’s what Timothy and I were doing when we were suddenly called to guard duty along the flight line. And while we were out there on guard duty, not a single Russian dared attack our base!

After several months of pounding the typewriter, I got word of an opening in the 50th Tactical Fighter Wing Information Office. They needed an enlisted man who could write, not just type. I applied and got the job. So at that point I became a journalist. At first my task was simply to edit and re-type stories others had written for our base weekly newspaper, the Hahn Hawk. I desperately wanted to do reporting and writing, but I had the misfortune of working for 1st Lieutenant Stanley Rodman. He was a Yale graduate (and triply proud of that fact), and he told me straight-out, “You are not qualified to write. You are an enlisted man!” That deflated my sails for a while, but one thing about the Air Force life is this: if you learn to wait a bit, either you or the someone you don’t like will be posted elsewhere. Rodman left soon enough, and he was replaced by a Captain Bud Roth. Turns out Roth wanted little to do with the “writing” of the stories but rather with the managing of the office and the conduct of public affairs. That was my chance. I worked with a non-com by the name of Master Sergeant Bud Nelson and soon became sports editor and later assistant editor. As for Rodman? I never saw him again. But I truly wished for that opportunity! I wanted that snot-nosed college graduate to know that after his departure, the enlisted man who “could not write” had won five consecutive quarterly awards for journalistic excellence in competition with 28 other command weekly newspapers. Rodman had won but one or two of those while he was at Hahn.

Before I move on with reminiscing about Hahn and the Cold War, I should here mention something else about Captain Bud Roth. He was the first commissioned officer I had met who had been an enlisted man for many years (roughly ten) before gaining his commission via OCS (officer candidate school). I would be remiss not to mention that he inspired me to do likewise. I did "likewise" only four years after leaving Hahn.

But 1963 at Hahn Air Base soon became about much more than outdoing Rodman (the writing). Two more life-changing events would happen before the year ended. Near the end of October I met a young lady whose name I learned only after "proper" introduction. That proper introduction was performed by Frau Elfriede Fink, our office community relations advisor (and it cost me a pack of Pall Mall cigarettes – which at the time went for 13¢). The young lady was Josefine Lohse. After exchanging names (in my office where she had come to pick up the Hahn Hawk newspaper), I asked her out to a Halloween event some of the fellows in the headquarters were planning. She said she'd "ask her father." We did go out on October 31, but the original plan had fallen by the wayside so we went to dinner at Bernkastel on the Mosel River. We ate at the Ratskeller Restaurant on the town square. And the rest – as one often hears – is history, and the making of a separate book.

Less than a month after our first date, the Cold War came again to "heat up." It was November 22, 1963, and I happened to be in Berlin. That evening (Germany time) a pocket-sized transistor radio carried the report. President John Fitzgerald Kennedy had been killed in Dallas. The world froze. No one knew the who or the why of it all. But suspicious heads turned toward Moscow. The military went to readiness status not unlike that of the Cuban Missile Crisis. Berlin – I was at Tempelhof Air Base – hunkered down. Now when you're an American military man "hunkered down" in Berlin, the Cold War seems anything but cold. Berlin was deep within Eastern Germany (a.k.a. the Russian zone). American forces in Berlin were surrounded by 21 Soviet divisions. Any outbreak of warfare would result in utter annihilation of the small "trip wire" contingent of Americans in Berlin. Since I was from Hahn Air Base, I had just become part of that tripwire. But not being directly assigned to any unit in Berlin, I took advantage of being "stranded" and walked the streets of Berlin. I observed the Berlin reaction to the killing of an American President. And not just any American President, but one who had visited Berlin and sparked the enthusiasm of Germans in the city not only when he said, "Ich bin ein Berliner" but also when he challenged those in the world who claimed not to grasp the real dangers of communism. To those Kennedy said, "There are some who say that communism is the wave of the future. Let them come to Berlin." So what I saw in Berlin those days following Kennedy's death was deep grief for a world leader they had seen as the hope for a free Berlin, a free Germany. I wrote an article. I wrote about processions throughout the streets of the city - about the size of Chicago - and signs and banners, and white candles burning in virtually every window, candles by the thousands upon thousands. Framed photos of Kennedy in home, store, and business windows everywhere. Long lines to sign books of remembrance (which were later forwarded to Jacqueline Kennedy). In bars and restaurants throughout the city, juke boxes were unplugged and turned to face the wall. Along the Berlin Wall, a small memorial cross to Peter Fechter, an 18-year-old killed while trying to escape from behind the Berlin Wall. The youth's memorial cross at the foot of the wall -

on the west side - bore an additional floral wreath with this inscription: John F. Kennedy was our friend.

With all of this, and more, how could I, an American airman just twenty years old, not be affected by such an outpouring of love and grief for my President? At the time, I remember wondering how many Americans would behave similarly if they learned of the death of the German Chancellor, Kenney's counterpart. Would many even know his name? I knew his name, and his nick-name and had actually met the man face-to-face! (Another story, perhaps later in this piece.) So for me being in Berlin at that moment in history was a searing experience.

Weeks later, back at Hahn Air Base, I re-united with Josefine. We dated. We became engaged. We married. In April, 1964. And I was still half-a-year shy of 21. Now I don't wish to short-change the stories of our early relationship, our early married years, and the start of our family. For that may be another memorial book. So, I'll return now to the Hahn AB years.

As an Airman Second Class I had lived in the barracks directly across the street from the 50th Tactical Fighter Wing headquarters building where I worked. Marriage meant moving out and setting up on one's own, so Josefine and I rented a one-room "apartment" which was actually naught but a spare room in a village farmer's house. We shared a bathroom with the landlord's family. By mounting a ceiling-to-floor curtain, we divided the room. With that we could call the place a one-bedroom studio apartment. My working life on base remained much the same as it had been - it was actually a truly fun job - but living in a quaint

German farming village was a veritable learning experience. At the time I spoke only a handful of German words and phrases. More to add to the learning curve! I'll add just an anecdote or two here just to offer a bit of the "flavor" of my new village life.

I had already discerned that the village folk did not take a daily bath! That was an event generally scheduled only for Saturdays. So, after a few days I began to feel a bit "ripe" and decided to give it a try - to take a bath, that is. Wrapped only in a towel, I headed for the shared "family" bathroom serving our "one-bedroom studio apartment." Though the bathroom was somewhat rustic in accoutrements, it looked simple enough. There was a tub. Directly above and behind the tub was a water heater. So far so good. I turned the faucet "on" and began to fill the tub. Ice cold water emerged. Wait a bit, I thought. It'll warm up. Wrong! So I examined the water heater. Must be a switch somewhere. Aha! Down near the bottom of the water heater I spotted a door about the same size as a car's fuel-tank door. Aha, I surmised. Behind that door will be a switch. Wrong again. But what I did see behind that door was the clue that explained how the system worked. Ashes! The bathtub's water heater was, indeed, a bit rustic. I'd need to build a fire! Time to go see the landlord. Dressing quickly, I went downstairs to find the landlord. In my best 20 or so German vocabulary words, I attempted to explain the dilemma. To this day I'm not quite sure what the landlord said to me, but I'm pretty sure he was telling me it wasn't Saturday. With that he led me out to the barn, showed me a pile of black briquettes each about half the size of a standard brick. He put a half-dozen or so into a bucket, handed it to me, then returned inside and gave me some matches! Lesson learned! And, no, I did not take a warm bath that day. My Mariposa days with my grandfather had taught me how to light a fire for our wood-burning stove. But lighting chunks of compressed coal is a much different challenge than igniting dry firewood. That was without a doubt the coldest - and quickest - bath I'd ever taken!

One additional anecdote will serve to add flavor to just how rustic that farming village was. On a Saturday morning, looking out the window, I noticed smoke. It was coming from a small stone structure I had seen in the middle of the village. I watched for a few minutes. The smoke was rising from a chimney. Aha! Then I saw a woman carrying a large tray enter the building. At this point Josefine began to wonder what had caught my attention. As I explained what I had just seen, she was amused. To her it was such a commonplace building with an equally commonplace purpose. She understood the rhythm of the village. I did not. She told me the building was a community oven. On Saturdays, one woman would light-up the wood-burning oven. Then, according to a monthly calendar within, village women would take their week's baking into the community oven. There they baked a week's supply of bread. And, of course, those delicious, flat "kuchen" which I had already learned were fresh and tasty and usually consumed with Sunday coffee at about 3 p.m. So, with that, I began to learn the rhythm of the village.

As for our own rhythm, we managed much the way the villagers managed. Having no car, we traveled to and from our little village of Hirschfeld to Hahn Air Base by means of a German commercial bus. This wound its way through a couple of other villages and the small town of Buechenbeuren before reaching the base's main gate. We shopped in the base commissary. Fortunately, this was adjacent to the main gate. Whatever we bought, we carried. Onto the bus. Alas, that rule also applied to one other necessity: diesel oil. Our "kitchen" in the one-room apartment consisted of a shelf with sink along the rear wall, and a diesel-oil stove which heated our room and doubled as a cooking surface. So the 5-gallon "Jerry cans" we carried onto the bus were the source of heating and cooking fuel. In time, we managed to add a few pieces of furniture to our lodging, and eventually bought a car. This was a 1960 Nash Rambler I bought from a departing Air Force dentist. With that we were a bit more mobile.

Having a car meant we could visit Josie's Oma and other relatives who lived near Karlsruhe along the Rhein River. We even made the 6-hour journey north to visit Josie's parents who had moved to the small town of Ohrdorf in the state of Niedersachsen. Her father had obtained a better teaching position and had moved there shortly after we had married.

So, at Hahn, I had become a husband, a father (with the birth of daughter, Iris), and a member of an extended family, all of whom warmly welcomed me into their fold. I had also advanced in my writing career. As sports editor of the base newspaper, Hahn Hawk, I gathered the news, wrote articles, and assisted with the mechanics of publishing a weekly newspaper. For basketball, I was the team statistician. How better to get the facts? For boxing I was the announcer on the mike in middle of the ring introducing the gloved combatants. For football, I, with my trusty portable typewriter, was up in the press box overlooking the field. I actually composed the stories "real time" as the game was in progress. Once, while I was doing this, our vice wing commander performed a pre-game flyby. From the press box, I looked down into the cockpit as his F-100 Super Sabre roared low over the field. Our opponents were the Army team from Rhein Main, theretofore unbeaten. They "hit the turf" as the jet blasted just over their heads. They never recovered from that moment of fear. The Hahn team defeated them handily! Well, okay, I suppose the fact that our air base team had a quarterback and receiver/running-back fresh out of the Air Force Academy might have helped a bit. With Rich Mayo at quarterback and Mike Quinlan to rush and receive, that flyby might not really have been needed to secure victory. By the way, Mayo and Quinlan were pilots, duly and legitimately assigned to Hahn. So they were "legal" team members. They also flew the F-100 and would have wanted to do the flyby themselves if the vice wing commander had not out-ranked them.

With this you might get the idea that I really enjoyed my job at Hahn Air Base. I did! And looking back over my 24-year Air Force career that was without a doubt the most enjoyable "job" I had.

1966 On to Niagara Falls

Arriving at Niagara Falls Air Base, I was again tasked to produce a base newspaper – this time as editor. But, in reality I was reporter, photo editor, copy editor, and editor. And for those of you reading this who might not be aware of certain realities of an Air Force base, allow me to add this:

an Air Force base is much more than a location from which to launch aircraft. It is a community with families. There are fire fighters, policemen, grocery and retail stores (bx and commissary for short), mechanics, bankers, doctors and dentists, and yes, schools (at the overseas bases). There are churches, movie shows, and bowling alleys. So for purposes of informing, educating, and motivating, our bases have newspapers. Hence my job as journalist.

At Niagara Falls what little flying activity took place was done by a reserve unit flying the C-119 Flying Box Car. These shaky old beasts had history in the Korean War and in Vietnam. Mostly they were for cargo and troop transport. Some were outfitted as gunships. These were outfitted with side-firing weapons capable of firing up to 6,000 rounds per minute per gun. The "Boxcar" was also used for mid-air retrieval of space capsules returning to earth.

But my unit at Niagara was part of Air Defense Command. We were mostly concerned with radar coverage and a few Bomarc missiles. These fellows were "surface to air" missiles designed to bring down enemy aircraft. Why at Niagara Falls? Well, examine the geography, do the arithmetic, then call me if you need clarification.

Niagara was my first stateside assignment - other than the training bases at Lackland and Keesler. The tempo was far more relaxed than at bases overseas. So I had time to advance other aspects of my career. Namely education. Back at Hahn I had begun my college work. I had taken a 12 week "immersion" class in German and gained my first 12-semester-hours of college credits. So at Niagara I enrolled in evening classes at Niagara Community College and nabbed another dozen credits, these mostly in U.S. History. I also had time to earn a few more needed bucks. So, I worked the Friday and Saturday midnight-to-eight a.m. shift in a gas station. Talk about "burning the candle" at both ends! For more than a year I slept nary a wink from Thursday night to Sunday night. Had some interesting events at that gas station - an Atlantic Richfield station at 4th and Main. One night I sold scarcely a drop of gasoline. The police had blocked all streets owing to race riots (1967-1968 was a troubled time in our country. Google it, you'll find out why.) I could not close the station. There literally was no key. There also was no cash-register - just a well-worn drawer in an old wooden desk. And on all of my midnight shifts, I was the only person on duty. Pumping gas. Changing oil. Repairing tires. Replacing belts, hoses. Doing "lube jobs." One night I replaced all four tires on some lady's car, changed the oil, did a lube job, replaced the water-pump belt, replaced both the lower and upper radiator hoses, filled the gas tank - all while running out to the pumps and serving other customers. The lady's bill was over $300 and that was an all-time record for a midnight shift. Tony, the boss, was blown away when he came in at 8 a.m. to relieve me from my shift. Then there was the night of the drunk Indian. Long story. We'll save it for later.

Niagara was where Eric was born, so Iris had a little brother, and Josie had two young'ens to care for.

So between night school for college and night-shift for extra income, Niagara was a busy time. Oh, yeah, I did also work my daytime Air Force job. Most interesting interview was with a C-119 Flying Boxcar enlisted crewman. He was a reservist, and a somewhat elderly fellow. I did a story on him. He had been a survivor of the Bataan Death March. (Google that one!)

Norton Air Force Base, California, 1968-1969

One day at Niagara I got a phone call from Norton Air Force Base. Someone at the Air Force Inspector General office. I was invited to join their staff. To this day I don't know who exactly called, or why me? How would they have known about me? But they did and they asked for me by name. So, a month or two after that call, we were on our way to California. The Air Force Inspector General and Safety Center. These were the feared "I.G." inspectors who tested the readiness of Air Force bases worldwide. The Safety Center - these were the best-of-the-best pilots and crewmen who went to crash sites of Air Force planes and conducted investigations to seek causes. As for me? No base newspapers this time! Now I was a historian of this top-level Air Force organization. I and one civilian wrote one classified and one unclassified history book each six months. I was good at making deadlines. The civilian, Fran Fowler, was a superior writer. He had trouble with deadlines. We both worked for Lt Col Ellis Frady. He hated missing deadlines.

But LtCol Frady was a man with heart of gold toward those who did not miss deadlines. And even before I met the man, I had earned that heart of gold without so much as knowing it. We had arrived in San Bernardino in time for breakfast. Having overnighted in Needles, California, that final day of cross-country driving was a short one. We had planned it that way. From Niagara Falls to San Bernardino in those days was some 2,800 miles. We had hit the road the same day as the moving van had pulled away from our home in Niagara Falls. We unknowingly beat the truck to San Bernardino by one day. So, at breakfast, we picked up a local newspaper and searched the ads for a place to live. We found a nice new apartment complex just a mile or two from where we were eating. We liked it, signed a contract, paid the rent, and headed to Norton AFB with the door key in my pocket. At Norton we checked in to spend the night in the on-base quarters. It was then about noon. So I picked up the phone and called the transportation office to advise them we had arrived and had an address for delivery of our furniture. They responded that our truck was arriving the next morning and would proceed directly to our new apartment. They would off-load the furniture at 9 a.m. saving the trouble and expense of off-loading into temporary storage, which would have been the normal procedure. So we were set.

Next I called my new office and was put directly through to LtCol Frady. He welcomed us, asked where we were, and said, “I’ll be right over” after I told him we were at the non-com temporary lodging. He showed up within minutes. We shook hands, he inquired how the family was after such a long trip, and then he said, “You’ll need a week or so to get squared away. Find a place to live. Get your furniture, and all that.” I told him we already had an apartment, and the moving van would off-load our furniture “tomorrow at 9 a.m.” He was totally dumbfounded. I thought he was about to choke on his own astonishment. “Well, when did you arrive?” he asked. “This morning about 8 a.m.” I said. After explaining about breakfast, the newspaper ad, the apartment and my call to transportation, I said we'd be staying just this one night in non-com lodging.

I saw nothing unusual about it all. He, on the other hand ... well, you could have pushed him over with a feather. "You are a Tiger!" he shouted. And from that day, I was his Tiger. LtCol Ellis Frady must have spent the rest of that day bragging up and down the hallways of the I.G. and Safety building about his new Staff Sergeant. By the time I arrived the day after taking delivery of our furniture, every soul I met already knew me as "Tiger."

So, for the next year-and-a-half I was Staff Sergeant Tilton, a.k.a. "Tiger." I worked within a windowless building, a converted long warehouse (neither the first nor the last of those during my Air Force career) and compiled and wrote history books. At Norton I had no time for evening or weekend jobs, but I did continue the evening college classes, this time at San Bernardino Valley College. There I took courses in Geology, Algebra, Public Relations, and English. Also, by this time Josie's English had advanced to the point that she could seek employment. She took a weekend job at a local restaurant, a cafeteria place called "George's." So, we were busy raising our family, working, and yes, finally meeting some of my family in California.

Being at the I.G. headquarters had another singular advantage. Just down the hall from my office was the most complete library of Air Force regulations on the planet. I was able to research through them at will. And I did. Remembering Captain Roth at Hahn Air Base, I searched the "regs" until I found all the requirements and procedures for me to apply for commissioning as an officer. I applied as soon as I had accumulated enough college credits, and with the complete backing of LtCol Frady my application sailed straight up the chain of command to Frady's boss, a Major General, and from there to Air Force Headquarters in Washington D.C. Frady pushed for his "Tiger" - even though it meant he would lose me from his staff. And, by the summer of 1969, Josie, Iris, Eric and I packed up and left San Bernardino. Josie and the kids went to stay the summer with her parents in Germany while I launched into my courses at the University of Nebraska, Omaha.

Omaha, Nebraska, 1969-1970

My Air Force job in Omaha was to be a college student. I had qualified for what was called the Bootstrap program. In a single calendar year at the University of Nebraska, Omaha, I took 48-semester-hours of courses. That was what remained to be completed if I was to graduate with a bachelor's degree and qualify for Officer Commissioning School. That was 12-credits in the summer of 1969 followed by two semesters of 18-credits each leading to graduation in May, 1970. In September, 1969, Josie, Iris, and Eric returned from Germany and joined me in Omaha. She got a waitressing job not far from the university. I was with the kids evenings (lots of playtime), and after they were tucked-away sleeping, I had plenty of time for studies. After graduation, we returned to San Bernardino, rented yet another apartment and returned to work with LtCol Frady at the I.G. while I awaited "orders" for Texas for officer training. During those few weeks I was promoted to Tech Sergeant - that's E-6 to you non-Air Force wonks! Soon thereafter, wearing those five stripes on my sleeves, I headed off to San Antonio and Officers Commissioning School. Josie and the kids remained behind in California.

San Antonio, 1970

It was my second assignment to San Antonio. I had been there 9 years earlier as an Air Force basic trainee. Oh, how different it was this time! I was a non-com rather than a "rainbow," and I was an officer candidate. But don't get the idea it was a cake-walk. Far from it. All of my fellow candidates were college graduates, so the competition was intense. What was most difficult, though, was being "commanded" and "inspected" by upper classmen whose entire Air Force career consisted of the six weeks they had spent as lower classmen. Those of us "new" lower classmen who had been non-coms really had to grit our teeth. Each of us had about 10 years of "real" Air Force under our belts. We resented the "smart-ass" almost-lieutenants who were our quasi senior officers. But, because we knew we were on "TDY" – temporary duty assignment – we knew we could tough it out. And we did. So we marched, we ran mile-after-mile, we attended classes, we fired weapons, and after twelve hot summer weeks, we graduated. We were lieutenants. Very experienced lieutenants.

Josie flew down to San Antonio for my commissioning. Then we returned to San Bernardino, packed up once again, and headed off to the next assignment.

Indianapolis, 1970

More training. At Indianapolis I was again a student. This time as a commissioned officer among other commissioned officers. The school was Defense Information School, DINFOS for short. I spent ten weeks learning, for the most part, what I had already practiced for ten years as an enlisted man - the techniques of journalism. Were it not for the courses in radio and television broadcasting and public affairs I would have been bored. We lived in an apartment south of Fort Benjamin Harrison; Iris began her school life with a kindergarten class within walking distance of the apartment. Josie made the apartment our home as much as she could, but without or usual household items. Those items, including virtually all of our furniture, kitchenware, and clothing were in storage until we moved to a permanent assignment following the ten weeks at DINFOS. We made do with what little we had brought along in the car. We bought Swanson TV-dinners in small aluminum trays which were divided into sections for potatoes, vegetables, and the meat entree. We washed and saved the aluminum trays. And it was good we did. For at Thanksgiving that year I invited three Vietnamese officers to our apartment to share our Thanksgiving meal. They were foreign-officer students attending the same course I was taking. Two were Vietnamese Army lieutenants and one was a captain in the Vietnamese Air Force. Josie had managed to roast the traditional turkey and prepare all the traditional trimmings. We taught our visitors what to do with the wishbone. They sang a festive Vietnamese song while the captain played his guitar. It was a memorable Thanksgiving meal. Made all the more so by the fact that we dined using our collection of Swanson aluminum trays. Our guests didn't mind. They understood the transient nature of a military life. I, and they, graduated from the

Public Affairs Officers Course just a day before Christmas. To this day I know nothing of their fate in the war which was at the time ravaging their country and to which they had to return. As for us, we loaded our 1967 Chevy (bought at the time I was pumping fuel and servicing cars in Niagara Falls) and hit the road. Next destination - Great Falls, Montana. My first "real" assignment as a lieutenant.

1970 – Christmas on the Road

As we set out from Indianapolis that Christmas of 1970, we had already driven four coast-to-coast cross-country trips. Nearly 12,000 miles in all. Such was the nature of an Air Force life. And most of this driving was before the introduction of interstate highways. We knew the famed Highway 66 oh so well. From the East Coast to the Pacific, over the Rockies four times. Oklahoma, Texas, and all the desert states. We had experienced a flat tire while pulling a U-Haul trailer in Wyoming, the loss of a transmission (in our old Rambler) as we came down out of the Colorado Rockies, and being - literally - shot at while on a highway in Ohio (a carload of crazies at a time of civil discord). So we were well beyond being rookies as we took to the highway and headed for Montana and a base called Malmstrom AFB. We had developed a daily travel plan, this out of necessity as we traveled five to six hundred miles a day with two children in the rear seat. (This was before the days of seat belts and toddler car seats a la Graco and Cosco.) We had filled the rear with pillows and blankets such that we made a fully level but protected area behind the front car seat. (This was made both safer and easier in those days owing to another "old-fashioned" quirk. The front seat in those days was one long "bench.") We packed the car each night before bedtime and departed each morning at four a.m. with the kids still sleepy and in their pajamas. They readily fell back asleep, and that gave us three hours of good, low traffic, driving time before we stopped at 7 a.m. for breakfast. Then we'd get another good three-hour run with the kids playing on their in-car playground. At 11, we'd stop. Get out walk around. Play in a park. Eat lunch around noon. And then drive to 3 p.m. It was not at all difficult to find a "vacancy" at a motel that early in the afternoon. And with either a bathtub or a swimming pool, depending on season, we'd have wash-up and play time. Followed by dinner. Followed by re-packing the car. Followed by the same routine the next day.

Such was our routine as we left DINFOS and Indianapolis behind. That first day we drove to Peoria, Illinois, and spent Christmas Eve. To this day we remember that meal. The hotel we picked (more or less by chance) just happened to have a German chef by the name of George. And he was a "chef" in every sense of the word. He was on duty even though the place was nearly empty (no surprise given the date). Every morsel of every dish and side-dish was delicious to the point of scrumptious. And Chef George came and sat with us and chatted with us about how he started every day at the market seeking out the freshest of everything. What a meal! What a memory. It was Christmas after all!

Three days later we arrived in Great Falls, Montana. We had lost a few hours and added an unexpected overnight as we crossed the border out of Wyoming just north of Sheridan. Bad luck. We lost a fuel pump in our 67 Chevy. Good luck. We coasted downhill a couple of miles directly into the parking lot of a nice, warm, rustic motel. More good luck. I wandered by foot into town and located a Cheyenne Indian auto mechanic. (Note: We were at the small town of Lodge Grass, just a stone's throw from the Little Bighorn Battlefield. Remember General Custer?). The Indian and I worked together, in the dark, in 21-degree, windy weather, on the ground, under the car. We took out the broken fuel pump. Telephoned a parts shop in Sheridan, 40 miles behind us back in Wyoming. Arranged for the pump to arrive on the next Greyhound bus and installed the new pump the next morning. This, too, is all part of an Air Force career!

1971, Malmstrom Air Force Base

With the Cold War still very much ongoing, and the Vietnam War raging, I found myself assigned to NORAD's 24th Air Division. This was my first non-training assignment as an officer. Air defense was our division's task. We had to be able to see the "enemy" and we had to be able to destroy him. To do this, our air division was equipped with layers of radar systems reaching far up into Canada, and we had, at various locations, fighter-interceptor aircraft, primarily the F-106 Delta Dart. One of our division units flying this aircraft was the 5th Fighter Interceptor Squadron, then located in North Dakota at Minot Air Force Base.

I actually flew in one of these. Key word there was "in." Remember, the Air Force in its wisdom never intended me to be a pilot. But there is a two-seat model of the F-106 (or, there was in 1971 at any rate). I needed to get "down" to Colorado Springs, our command headquarters, and so did a certain pilot. So I got the rear seat! We made the trip in a few minutes less than an hour. *(A couple of years later I would drive that very route with my '67 Chevy. That trip took 14 hours.) Along the way we plummeted from FL 37 to - well, I'm not at liberty to say how low, but I got a great view of the Yellowstone River and portions of Yellowstone National Park! So that ride was one of the highlights of my assignment at Malmstrom. There were others.

Unlike Niagara Falls - which, incidentally, was also an Air Defense Command unit - Malmstrom was what you might call a "full service" base. The host unit was a Strategic Air Command missile wing. This unit operated underground ICBM launch facilities scattered all about the state of Montana. These intercontinental ballistic missiles were ready to strike enemy targets anywhere in the world. Talk about Cold War! My unit, the 24th Air Division, was a part of NORAD which was both a multi-service and multi-national command with the result that my boss was a U.S. Army lieutenant colonel. LtCol Paul Hinkin was one of the finest men I have ever had the pleasure of knowing, and he was a superb boss. Since our unit was comprised of radars and fighter interceptors (like the F-106 I flew "in"), and since many of those were in North Dakota, Canada, and Montana, I traveled extensively. I would go out to inspect and assist our public affairs offices, and I would write articles for our division monthly magazine. Our extended radar units sent their real-time "picture" of thousands upon thousands of square miles of flying space to our division headquarters at Malmstrom. We could "see" every aircraft - civilian, commercial, or military - flying anywhere within our region, and that included the northernmost parts of Canada. Our division's data was forwarded to Colorado

Springs, Colorado, where it was combined with similar data from other regions. There, deep within Cheyenne Mountain, all such data was combined and was displayed on a screen half the size of a football field. Every flying object over the northern half of the U.S. and all of Canada could be seen and tracked! It was all to provide early warning and rapid response for a Soviet air or nuclear attack.

While assigned to the 24th at Malmstrom, I was sent to Denver, Colorado, to be trained for a "secondary" career area. (All officers were trained in both primary and secondary careers). My secondary was to be Disaster Preparedness. The emphasis was upon recovery from and return to mission-readiness after nuclear attack. In short, I was trained to prepare for and clean up from nuclear, chemical, or biological contamination. That course lasted several weeks. (More about that follows below.) Upon return to Malmstrom, my commander called upon me for a special mission. Two of our non-coms –one Canadian and one American – had been trout fishing up on the Missouri River at the face of Holter Dam. Witnesses had seen them get caught-up in a whirlpool, fall from their boat, and disappear beneath the water. I was sent to head up a combined military/civilian search team. We spent about a week at the task. On the third day we found the body of the American, more than a mile downstream from the face of the dam. We continued searching. We asked the power production people at the dam (it was one of a series of hydro-electric power plants along the upper Missouri River) if they could reduce the flow of the water in the hope of finding the other victim. They did so but had first to close two other upstream dams in order to reduce Holter dam's flow without causing flood damage. Even with the reduced flow (and better fishing for a handful of anglers at the face of the dam), we did not find the missing Canadian. His body resurfaced a few weeks later. It had been snagged in construction debris at the face of the dam all that time.

For most of my assignment at Malmstrom, I was writing for magazines and traveling to and from our far-flung units. But one day an F-106 crashed onto a Montana wheat ranch. I was tasked to join the staff of the crash investigation team. This was partly because I was an officer who could write, and partly because my final assignment as an enlisted man was with Air Force Safety and Inspection Center back at Norton. That center at Norton was the central Air Force agency responsible for investigation and research into crashes of Air Force aircraft. As a result of my work there as historian, I was familiar with the process and much of the terminology. So when the accident investigation team formed at Malmstrom, I became its recorder. I wrote portions of the final report, revised other portions, assembled all documentation, and prepared the final document which would ultimately land on someone's desk back at Norton. It was an extremely interesting task. This crash near Malmstrom – as with any crash in the world -- had to be exhaustively studied so as to determine the cause. Much is at stake. If a crash is the result of pilot error, the Air Force may find a need to revise pilot training. If a crash results predominantly from mechanical failure, the aircraft industry itself may need to modify current or future aircraft of the same type. So every piece must be located and analyzed.

Our team had specialists for the overall F-106 aircraft itself, others for the Pratt and Whitney engines, still others for the aircraft's fire control system (components which assist the aircraft and its pilot in locating and destroying a target.) The team had mechanical engineers, communications specialists, maintenance officers, and various operational experts. That's why I found my task to be so interesting and challenging. The pilot himself might be facing termination of his career. The manufacturer might be facing termination of contract, not to mention a host of legal issues. Other pilot and crew lives were at stake as well!

In this case, the pilot had stated he had experienced an on-board fire while at 37,000 feet. He had exhausted all efforts to control the aircraft and had ejected. Parts of his account of events were doubted by certain members of the team who initially thought the pilot had erred and had not followed correct procedures. After well over a month of investigating every aspect of the crash (all the pieces – thousands of such – were collected and spread out in a hangar) ultimately the pilot's version of the problem was borne out. A single flange along a fuel line had been examined in a lab at Kelly AFB, Texas. The metal flange had shown certain crystallization characterization which could have occurred only at or above 35,000 feet where oxygen levels are lower. This confirmed the pilot's claim as to when the fire started. Such crystallization could not have been the case for a post-crash fire at surface-level owing to higher concentration of oxygen. Case closed. Pilot's career continued. Flange modification directed.

For me, as recorder, it was the learning experience of a lifetime. Truly a highlight of my first assignment as a commissioned officer. All that, and I was still a 2nd Lieutenant!

There were numerous other tasks and challenges yet to be faced at Malmstrom. After all, both the Cold War and the Vietnam War remained the "mission." So after the crash was all cleaned up, so to speak, I was sent off to Denver, Colorado, for some specialized training at Lowry AFB. Not unlike the other services, Air Force officers are trained to perform in more than one career field. My alternate career field turned out to be something called Disaster Preparedness. Yes, portions of that included learning how to prepare for such emergency situations as hurricanes and earthquakes. But the core of my course was conducted at a place called Rocky Mountain Arsenal just east of the Denver area. I was trained in methods of decontamination when faced with chemical, biological, and radioactive agents. The idea is to "clean up" people and equipment from such agents so we can return our forces to an operational status following attack. One example will suffice here. I learned how to self-inject an agent called atropine to help reduce the effects of exposure to sarin (nerve gas). So, yes, we trained with gas masks, protective suits and such things. On the nuclear warfare side we trained to minimize the effects of (or clean up) such things as radioactive alpha and beta particles. Not much we could do about gamma rays as those guys are gone before you knew they were there! So, lots of useful training. The good news is I never had to put that training to use. Not while I was in the Air Force anyway. But I was able to use portions of that training in my post-Air Force career to help my school district In Carmel, Indiana, plan for disaster response following the 9/11 attacks. But that was my second career. The teaching career. Another book? Maybe later.

Back at Malmstrom following the disaster response training, I had scarcely unpacked my travel bags (laundry needed, you know) when my Norad commander decided I was the perfect choice to head up a search and rescue mission on the upper Missouri River. Two of our non-coms had been reported missing at the face of Holter Dam. They had last been seen struggling with a whirlpool at the face of the dam. I worked for two weeks with a local sheriff. His team and mine searched both sides of the river downstream from the dam. On day three we recovered one body. The American. Still missing was the Canadian. We worked with the power utility company operating the dam and arranged to have the flow shut down in an effort to recover our second non-com. This required shutting down two other dams upstream, each in turn, before we could hope to reduce the flow at Holter Dam. That done, we continued our search. It was great for the trout fishermen on the river. Less water. Greater concentration of fish. But our task was grisly. No fishing for us. Alas, we did not find the Canadian. The upstream flow of water had to be released lest damage occur. I left the site, but returned two weeks later when the Canadian's bloated body came to the surface. It had been entangled in submerged construction debris. Such ended the search mission.

But most of my duties at Malmstrom were the writing and publishing of Air Force magazine articles, and the travel to distant places such as Grand Forks, North Dakota, and, oh yes, to the bright, white beaches of Florida where I wrote and produced a special edition of our magazine dedicated to something we called "William Tell" -- an air-to-air weapons meet. Think of this as a sort of a "shoot-out in the sky" involving the best and the hottest of aircraft and pilots in a week-long competition mostly flown over the waters of the Gulf of Mexico. My magazine (for the 24th Norad Region) documented the event, and if memory serves, one of our squadrons won the "shoot-out" while pilots, load crews, and maintenance teams honed their combat skills. That magazine caught the attention of my headquarters (Air Defense Command and Norad) and may have played a role in my re-assignment to Colorado Springs, my next assignment. (Life lesson here: Be careful about doing something too well; it might get you a promotion to somewhere you don't want to go.)

Late 1972, Ent Air Force Base

After scarcely two years in Montana – a place we had come to truly appreciate both for the work environment and the great outdoor life – I had done so well that the headquarters noticed. Off to Colorado Springs! I found myself assigned to Hq Air Defense Command. Here I worked as part of a large staff of public affairs officers. We churned out magazine articles and fed news releases to the media. I worked on occasion – but not with regularity – inside the Norad complex in Cheyenne Mountain. For the most part my desk inside a windowless behemoth of a building called the Chidlaw was the scene of drafting, editing, and re-drafting of staff papers, memos, and news releases. My boss back at Great Falls had been distressed to see me go to the Hq. He was an Army lieutenant colonel – Paul Hinkin by name – and was without question the finest officer for whom and with whom I worked at any time during my 24-year career. He had hinted I might not like working at the Hq. And he was right. I was a very junior lieutenant hidden among captains, majors, lieutenant colonels, and colonels. Still, the Colorado Springs assignment was a time of learning and a time when I saw the winding down of the Vietnam War. Several of my fellow staff members played an active part in the 1973 return to the U.S. of our former prisoners of war in Operation Homecoming. While they were away, I keep "their desks" and mine fully engaged in the routine work of the Hq. Then, after about two years, there came an opportunity for me (and Josie and the kids, of course) to return to Germany. But first. The deal wouldn't be sealed until I agreed to a remote, one-year assignment. Next stop, Thule, Greenland.

Mid 1974, Thule, Greenland

If you really want to know more about my Thule assignment, the best thing to do is read this novel: *The Qanaq Conundrum* Kindle Edition, by Frank Tilton which is online as an Amazon Kindle and paper-back book. Sure, it's fiction. But most of it is also true and will give you a pretty good idea what a year at Thule is like. For starters, Thule is so far north that 99.9% of the earth is south. We were about as close to the North Pole as any human ought to be. There were long periods of 24-hour darkness and long periods of 24-hour daylight. Only in late March and late September was there an even daily distribution of light and dark. The base was nestled close to the edge of the great Greenland icecap. In fact, I went up onto it a few times. Just past Camp Tuto, an abandoned Army support base for Camp Century. I also visited Eskimo villages. Places called Siorapaluk, Qanaq, Moriusaq, Qerqertoq, and Savissivik. These were Greenlandic Eskimo villages north and northeast of Thule. Qanaq was the village we Americans had displaced when the base was built. We flew in by helicopter and delivered food, medicine, mail, and – at Christmas season – Santa's gifts for the children. On one of these trips in December (24-hour darkness) the Eskimos used 55-gallon oil drums with burning oil lamps to mark out our landing pad. We additionally kicked out a flare which floated down via parachute for additional light. (No, I wasn't a pilot. The Air Force is a lot smarter than that, remember?) Once on the ground we paired up with Eskimos who led us up a trail to the village. I found myself trying to chat with my Eskimo companion, but he spoke no English, and I spoke no Greenlandic (a local branch of the Inuit language). So, I thought, "What the hey!" And I started speaking German to the Eskimo. It worked! Sort of. He understood me and responded in Danish. That was close enough to German that we were able to carry on a bit of conversation. Who da' thunk!? It worked because Danish is the official language of Greenland (government, business, education). Many Eskimos traveled to Denmark for advanced education. So, while at Thule I saw Eskimos, kayaks, dogs and sleds, and observed their daily life. I watched an Eskimo feed seal meat to his team of dogs, and while I did not face-to-face see a Polar bear, I did see Eskimos wearing polar bear pants. Aside from nylon rope, coffee, and Johnson outboard motors for their boats, they were a truly primitive hunter-gatherer culture. One thing of great interest I noticed was how they got fresh water. They drove a truck out onto the frozen bay (salt water) and located icebergs (from the glaciers of Wolstenhome Fjord and others like it). They used chain saws to cut up the icebergs (which were stuck for the winter) and took the fresh water ice chunks back to the village for melting.

There were a good many highlights to my year at Thule. In fact, as far as job satisfaction goes, Thule and Hahn Air Base were my favorite assignments. Both involved hands-on work using the tools of journalism. Unlike Hahn AB, though, where my newspaper - Hahn Hawk - was physically produced in a German civilian printing plant in Trier, my bi-weekly Thule paper was somewhat rudimentary in terms of production. It was totally an "in-house" product. Plenty of "hands-on." We used a sort of homemade offset printing method using lithograph masters. (Stone age stuff by today's standards.) It worked well enough, and we were able to write, do photography (two Danish guys in our photo lab), print and distribute the Thule Times. Our eager readers were a few hundred Americans - USAF - a couple hundred U.S. civilian contractors, and several hundred Danish civilians. There was plenty to write about at Thule. We were part of NORAD, the headquarters I had left behind in Colorado Springs. Our base was primarily concerned with detecting ballistic missiles that might be launched by our Cold War opponents. So, Thule had BMEWS -Ballistic Missile Early Warning System - radars with which we could notify NORAD if an attack was underway. There were also other types of tracking and telemetry devices that served related purposes.

My own job as information officer included the newspaper and a 24-hour radio and television station - American Forces Radio and Television Service. I had a crew of broadcast journalists who did daily news, sports, and entertainment broadcasting for our "northernmost" American forces. While I was there, I also found a way to take our radio-tv news feeds and from them print a daily paper we called World Wire. These we placed on tables in the dining hall which was one place all of us Thuleites would gather each day. By the way, all of the food was prepared by Danish cooks with much of the fresh food flown in weekly from Denmark. It was without a doubt the best "Air Force" food ever!

One memorable event I'll share before continuing this "Air Force Story" with my next assignment. Thule AB was located near the northernmost end of Baffin Bay and has surface access to the rest of the world via North Star Bay. But only in August and September when waters are "open" – that is, not frozen. It is just about the most remote place on the planet. And for that reason, it is surely the least likely place you'd expect to find an international "open" golf tournament. That is, until I got there. It turns out I am the originator of that tournament, and I recently learned that it continues now, more than forty years after I planned and "launched" that first tournament. Funnier still – I am not a golfer. Wasn't then, still am not. Here's the way it happened. It begins with what may be the most memorable landmark those who have spent time at Thule are likely to remember. Mt. Dundas. (See photo insert.) Said to be 750 feet in height, Mt. Dundas looks like one of those "mesa" mountains you might see in Utah or New Mexico. A flat, table-like top and sloping sides. From a distance is looks smooth. But up close it's rough and rocky. Very difficult walking. Now anyone who has spent a "summer" at Thule has climbed Mt. Dundas. I did so just days after arriving for my year at Thule, and with me was a group of newcomers including our new commander, Colonel Kleckner. He and I were on the edge of Mt. Dundas looking down to North Star Bay and it's icebergs.

I made some comment about a golf course called Pebble Beach Golf Course (not far from Monterey on California's coast). Klecker's response? "Tilton. Organize a golf tournament here." I did. The first tournament was July 19,1975. It was "open' because anyone could enter. Anyone, that is, who was legally at Thule. It was "international" because we had a Danish military commander as our liaison with Denmark, and local Danes could play. The rules? Well, Thule had only a handful of golf clubs thanks to some netting within our gymnasium which we called a driving range. So we had a drawing, both to see who could play, and to determine which club each player could use. Whatever club you "drew" was your one and only club for the tournament. Two more rules. You had to climb the mountain carrying three things. Your one club, some golf balls, and a small patch of carpet upon which to place your golf ball for each shot. Second rule? Your score was calculated by how many strokes it took you to land your ball within the "hole" which was actually a brightly painted circle of rocks approximately three feet in diameter. You'd understand the challenge if you saw the top of Mt. Dundas. It looked flat from a distance. But up close it was a rugged knee-banging surface difficult even to walk on. The good news? The weather cooperated. The tournament was a success. The bad news? I did not play. I was on crutches that day (and for several weeks). I had injured my knee in a volleyball game played the same afternoon I had climbed Mt. Dundas while preparing for the tournament. Oh, well. But, yes, I did create the tournament. See the July 25, 1975 issue of Thule Times.

Oh, and one other memorable event to share. While at Thule I needed yet some other activity to while away the many dark hours. So I taught a couple of college courses. Our base education office offered undergraduate courses as part of an extension campus for El Paso Community College of Colorado Springs. I taught freshman English 1 and also Introduction to Journalism. Both were three-semester-hour courses. And here's an unexpected result: One of my Thule students was a Master Sergeant by the name of LeFiebre. He was with the base hospital staff. My freshman English course was his first college credit. Years later in Germany – May of 1980 – I stood in a formation of U. of Maryland graduates as we became graduates. I had just completed my second bachelor's degree – this one in German. And standing right next to me, what a surprise! Sergeant LeFiebre, who had just completed his bachelor's degree – the one he started at Thule! I don't know who was more surprised. Neither of us (we were serving at different bases in Germany) knew that the other was graduating that day! To this day I count that event as a rarity. And it was a great memory of that year at Thule.

Mid 1975 to June 1981, Ramstein, a more active Cold War experience

The deal the Air Force personnel wonks had given me was that the Thule assignment – one year remote – would be followed by an assignment to Berlin. But someone manipulated things. I got Ramstein Air Base instead. So rather than risk losing both in a squabble with the HQs, off we went to Ramstein after returning to Colorado Springs just long enough to round up Josie and the young'ens. We arrived back in Germany in mid or late July, 1975, not quite ten years after departing Hahn AB for Josie's first trip to the U.S. I had left Hahn as a sergeant. I was returning to

Germany as a captain. That in itself is nothing to avoid boasting about. But the Ramstein assignment would turn out to be gut-wrenching in so many ways. I was assigned to Headquarters U.S. Air Forces in Europe which itself was the U. S. air component of NATO's forces, and the "Cold War" was neither finished, nor was it "cold." I found myself smack in the midst of the NATO vs. Warsaw Pact face-off. That upped the tempo for everything we did.

Like Colorado Springs, I was part of a large staff of public affairs officers, far too many of whom were busily preening themselves for their next promotion. That does not make for a pleasant working environment. I prefer to ask, "What is our task?" Too many of those guys ask, "Who is writing my evaluation?" Such things make a huge difference in the atmosphere of the work environment. The good news is, I did work with a few really fine officers. Guys like Larry Greer, Larry McCracken, and Fred Watkins. They, like me, are the type who are task-oriented and recognize that if the task goes well, the promotion will take care of itself.

For the first few months I was doing press releases to our "internal" audiences and overseeing 20 or so base newspapers (quality control and "policy" control). One of those papers was the Hahn Hawk. (That's where I had cut my teeth in journalism.) Some months later both I and Larry Greer were transferred out of "internal" and into Community Relations. This was a new branch of public affairs for me and though I was good at it, I did not enjoy it the way I had enjoyed journalism. As it turned out, "Com Rel" was not for the timid, the frail, or the weak of heart. In "Com Rel" as we called it, the writing was staff work. The task was "projects" and "events" instead of articles and headlines. We were constantly dealing with leaders (and their staffs) of foreign nations, with other European military forces, and with governmental officials throughout Germany. We sent airplanes to participate in air shows, and we planned both U.S. and allied participation in our own air shows. (For the next several paragraphs, I will be writing "we" for the simple fact that there are very few of these sort of things "I" did alone. That's the nature of staff work. But I would not be writing these things that "we" did if I did not have a major hand in it.) We set up air shows like the big one at Ramstein for the 1976 Bi-Centennial year. For that show we invited and worked the details to get six aerial demonstration teams to perform. Aside from the U.S.A.F. Thunderbirds, we pulled in similar teams from the U.K. and France, from Italy and Belgium, and from Canada. Just dealing with country clearances was a nightmare. Don't forget, the movement of aerial demonstration teams into and out of such air shows was, in fact, the movement of military forces across international borders. That meant approvals from every head of state and from their embassies. Not an easy task. At Ramstein that year we pulled in crowds in excess of 500,000 from virtually around the world. Who wouldn't want to see six teams like the Thunderbirds all in one day and at one base? We also got "weird" requests from the teams themselves, like this one from Italy. The Italian team - called the Frecce Tri Colori - flew an aircraft called the Fiat G91. It was a compact design fighter aircraft. So compact that the team leader did special on-site measurements of it, and then requested that they be allowed to fly one "through" an American C-5 Galaxy! That's right. Through. The Galaxy is so large, and it can be opened from both front and rear (while loading and off-loading). The Italians wanted to be the first to fly through it. They actually made the request, though we were never sure whether it was just in jest! But. With little delay we denied the request. But that ought to give you some idea of the range of things we "Com Rel" folks had to deal with.

Other "events" and "projects" I personally set-up, gained approvals for, and coordinated, included speeches by our generals at major events (some of these speeches I wrote), shipment of Air Force art displays throughout Europe, special briefings for members of European parliaments (see * and * *), U.S.A.F. participation in the Paris Air Show and the Farnborough Air Show, and performances of the U.S.A.F.E. Band throughout Europe (see* * *).

* Many of these briefings were dedicated to persuading European governments to approve the basing of new models of missiles within their borders. And, yes, they did approve. And, yes, that is one of the reasons the Cold War ended when it did. Also, one of these briefings was for members of the Parliament of Spain. I remember this one in particular for two reasons. One, we were attempting to convince Spain to join NATO. (And, yes, they did join. In 1982.) Two, I recall vividly what happened the day of their visit to Ramstein (for which I was the "Com Rel" project officer.) That day (Feb 23, 1981), while the group of 19 Spanish Parliamentarians was visiting us and receiving briefings, their very Parliament was attacked: about 200 soldiers and members of the paramilitary Civil Guard stormed the lower house of the Spanish Parliament, the Cortes, firing automatic weapons and shouting orders. They took hostage about 350 MPs debating a new government. We quickly adjusted our program so that our

visitors could stay in contact with their fellow MP's at home. As noted elsewhere, I was not the only person of our staff or our command to be involved. But I was in it up to my neck. The "project folder" was squarely on my desk!

** Here was another "event" involving Spain. It was a Saturday morning. You see, each of us staff officers would spend one week performing an early morning chore known as "duty officer." And that week included both Saturday and Sunday. Moreover, each day of "duty officer" week started at 5 a.m. The first chore of each day was to report to the "comm center" – a small single-story building near, but not attached-to, the headquarters. We would pick up a sizeable stack of printed messages that had arrived during the night. These we would take to our office for sorting and assembling into a morning briefing book for the colonel. Woe to the duty officer who did not adequately "brief" the colonel before staff meeting!

So, as it happened, I was on Saturday duty. It is the task of the duty officer to solve any problem that arises, or to have the wisdom to know when and whom to call for help. A ringing phone was never good news (much like that 5 a.m. steel whistle back in the days of basic training.) That's probably why to this day I tend to tense up and detest a ringing phone. But this time when I answered the phone I found myself up to my ears in curiosity and wonder. The kind of "wonder" like, "I wonder what I can do about this." On the other end of the call was a woman in Spain. She was the director of the zoo in Madrid. She wasted no time, in perfect English, explaining to me what she needed. A mother bear had given birth and the tiny cub would soon die – within hours – if we could not find a source of bear milk. Mama bear, for reasons not clear, would not, or could not, feed the cub. The zoo director asked if I could find some specially-formulated bear milk somewhere within Germany and have our Air Force fly it to Madrid. The short of it is yes, I did find the milk, and yes, I did have it flown to Madrid, but not via military aircraft. We found a civilian air carrier for that task.

At this point I cannot blame you if you're thinking "Come on. This can't be true." And looking back I sometimes have the same feeling. There were a good many fortuitous circumstances that came into play that day. The fact that I could speak German and just happened to be on duty that Saturday surely helped. The fact that I recognized that businesses in Germany on Saturday are (or were so then) open only until noon also helped. It also imposed a tight deadline. And the fact that I remembered often seeing a major dairy producer along the highway as we had often traveled to visit family in the north of Germany. I called that dairy products company, telephonically navigated through their staff, and lo and behold, did find a section that produced a specialized bear milk. I then became a go-between connecting them with the Madrid zoo director, and within three hours had the milk on the way to Spain. All this with no internet! Of interest, as I write this, and even with the internet, I cannot find that dairy products company. Perhaps it has been bought, sold, merged, and swallowed up. But, I did have success that day. And I did receive a photo of the bear baby and an invitation to visit the Madrid zoo. Alas, even those documents have evaporated over the years. Only memory remains at this time. And even that is fading.

***Once, to give you an idea of the complexity of arranging performances of the U.S.A.F.E. Band, I became a key player in this entanglement. It was 1976, America's Bicentennial Year. I was working a request from the U.S. Ambassador to Moscow. He wanted a unit of our band to perform for the July 4th celebration of America's 200 years of independence. Transporting an American military band from Germany into Russia during the Cold War was no simple task. After all, the band, as noted earlier, is a uniformed military unit. It was a multi-faceted and complex task, but it was moving along smoothly as such things go. All the signatures and approvals were falling into place. We had tasked an aircraft and everything looked great. Right up to but not beyond July 3rd. With less than 24-hours to go, the Russians notified us that they had approved the flight for the band, but they had not done so for the equipment. The equipment would have to go by train and be inspected by Russian forces both upon departure from Germany and upon arrival in Moscow. At the last minute we were forced off-load the band equipment from our aircraft. The Russians had kicked us in the kiester, so to speak. No way could we get the equipment to Moscow in less than 24-hours. Egg on face! The upshot was we did provide music for our Ambassador's Bicentennial event. Our band members hummed. One or two sang. And we got coverage in Time magazine. Egg on Russian faces.

One final "band" story before moving on. This one also involved Spain. And this one very nearly cost me my promotion to major. The task was to get the band to Spain (Torrejon Air Base) for a major change of command ceremony. Both the band and our 3-star vice commander were to board a C9 (the Air Force version of the Douglas DC9 aircraft) and fly to Spain. And rule-number-one is that one NEVER makes a general, regardless the number of stars, wait, or be late. To anything! Well, in the days leading up to this event I had been working scheduling events with the band. And when we discussed this particular flight we had agreed on all the details. Al, that is, but one. When we flew that band unit to its performance destinations, we often began the flight at Rhein Main AB, near Frankfurt. Other times we used Ramstein AB. Our "home" station. Somehow, I failed to specify which was the departure base. I probably assumed the band knew that with our 3-star boarding at Ramstein, so would the band. Murphy's law got me. big time! The day came. The general boarded. There was no band present at Ramstein. The aircraft departed with one very fuming-mad general and without the band. To shorten the story a bit, suffice it to say that my colonel (my boss) and the aircraft operations colonel, and the band commander, all managed to convince the really pissed-off general to allow the plane to return to Ramstein. The plane returned. The band and its equipment boarded. And I boarded that plane just before take-off with a hand-written note inside an envelope. I gave the note to the general's executive officer and explained orally that the fault was mine. I debarked the plane. It flew to Spain. But the story does not end there. I had known that such an event would launch a major investigation and that the "guillotine" would be readied. Heads would roll. Careers would end. And the most likely targets would be the guys in the operations staff with whom I worked on a regular basis. For starters they were physically and organizationally closer to the angry 3-star general. So when I "fessed up," they were spared. And it is good that they were spared. For things got worse, if that is even imaginable. You see, that same plane (the C9) was tasked for another flight that day. It was supposed to fly to Bonn, Germany, and pick up Helmut Schmidt and deliver him and his staff to a meeting in Berlin. Schmidt was Germany's Chancellor. The equivalent of President. Our planes routinely flew him to Berlin. This was so owing to Cold War agreements regarding access to Berlin. Complicated. But, there it was. My error not only pissed-off the very 3-star general who was directly in my chain of command, angered likewise a 2-star general at Torrejon, but also messed up a president's schedule.

And this happened just a few weeks before I was to depart from Ramstein for my next and final Air Force assignment in Indiana. Not only that, my records were in an office somewhere in the Pentagon where I was to be considered for promotion to major. Also, weeks later I learned who the president of that promotion board was. It was the same 3-star general I had so sorely pissed off that rueful day. And yet, before I departed Ramstein, my colonel told me the "rest of the story" (think Paul Harvey). Apparently, the 3-star general was so "blown away" -- as one says -- by my honesty in the face of certain personal disaster that he did not "red-line" my name from the list. I was promoted to major and that gold leaf was pinned on by my new commander at Fort Benjamin Harrison shortly after my arrival for duty.

So Ramstein was "gut-wrenching" in so many ways. It seemed I was forever being tasked to do the impossible. I was supposed to get airplanes to appear in air shows, though I did not "own" any airplanes or command any squadrons with airplanes; I was supposed to get the band to perform anywhere in Europe or North Africa, though the band and its commander did not work for me. I was supposed to get weighty displays of art from place to place though I had no transport unit at my command and no one to load or off-load the equipment much less set it up for display. Yes, it was a gut-wrenching assignment. And not all of the difficulties were at Ramstein Air Base, and not all of my tasks were done in the comfy environment of an office. Case in point: Egypt, 1979.

I found myself deployed to Egypt in late 1979. Now, this is a much bigger story than mine alone, so I will try to record for this "family" book only the part that I actually participated in. If you want more on the event itself, you can "Google" it as Operation Eagle Claw which actually took place April 24, 1980. This operation involved Army Delta Force and Rangers, some Air Force airlift units, and a Navy carrier wing. The "Eagle Claw" task was to rescue American hostages being held by Iran. My part of it began a couple of weeks before Christmas 1979. We still lived in Schrollbach, a village a few miles from Ramstein. As with other members of our public affairs staff, I would periodically be tasked to take the "deployment kit" home. This was a foot-locker filled with equipment and supplies essential to work in a remote location. I was at home with Iris and Eric while Josie was away in nearby Kaiserslautern getting some Christmas shopping done. We had a trip planned to spend Christmas holidays with Josie's parents in northern Germany (Hankensbuettel at that time). An Air Force blue station wagon appeared in front of our apartment. I knew immediately that our doorbell would ring. It did. I took the deployment foot locker and minimal clothing and departed after telling the kids to stay inside and wait for "Mommy" to return. We had no cell phones in those days, so Josie knew nothing of my departure until she faced a couple of crying, perplexed kids in the doorway. I had no way of knowing where I would be going or how long I'd be away.

I was delivered directly to the runway and in short order found myself aboard a small aircraft along with about 7 others, not counting the pilot and crew. From the operations building I had had just time to call my office, talk to the duty officer, and inform my boss that I had been picked up for deployment. Later I learned that not even my Ramstein boss knew where or why I had deployed. At the time only a small handful of "ops" folks in a tucked-away corner of our headquarters knew the what, the why, and the where. Five or six people. And their only line of communication was directly to the White House. No one else locally was aware. So aboard the aircraft were six people I had never before seen, and one colonel from our base in Lakenheath, U.K., whom I also did not know. The colonel told us nothing except to settle in and enjoy the flight. He said we'd land at Naval Air Station Sigonella, Sicily. We did. But we did not stay long. Just one overnight and a quick view of Mt. Etna, Europe's tallest active volcano. Just after sunrise, we (the same crew as the day before) boarded a C-141 Starlifter. It seemed to me to be a very large aircraft for so few people. After flying just an hour or so, more or less in the direction of Athens, Greece, our "colonel" stood up, reached into a pocket in his flight jacket, extracted an envelope, and approached the cockpit. In a minute or so, our plane noticeably changed its heading. Our colonel returned to the center of the aircraft and asked the six of us to gather around as he unfurled a map. He introduced himself with a bit more formality than we'd seen the day before. He was the vice wing commander at Lakenheath, he told us, and for this mission he would be our commander. He pointed to the open map and showed us a location in Egypt. He said it was an Egyptian base built by the Russians and that it would be our home for the foreseeable future. He began to give each of us assignments and told us what he expected to be done within the first two to three hours of our landing. Turning to me, he said I would be his "exec" and that there would be no public affairs work to be done. I was to be his admin guy, the personnel guy, and the get-it-done guy for whatever he needed. And so it was. Sitting on the floor of a C-141 and gathered around a map, I have to tell you, it felt like a scene from a movie. But it wasn't. It was real. And we'd soon be arriving in Egypt.

The short of it is that we did arrive in Egypt and immediately went about our various tasks. In a nut shell, we were to prepare ourselves and this rocky, remote airstrip to become operational. We would be living and working inside a crude concrete Russian-built aircraft shelter. We would be seeing C-141s coming and going, and when things were ready we'd be seeing an AWACS and its maintenance squadron arriving. The E-3 Sentry is an airborne warning and control system, or AWACS, aircraft. This plane was at that time (1979) one of the Air Force's newest combat tools having been operational for only about two years.

I stayed in Egypt for about six weeks until I was replaced by another member of my Ramstein AB office. And I did exactly what our colonel had asked, but I did find just a bit of "public affairs" work that I could do. Using a battery-operated radio from my deployment kit and a manual typewriter, I found that I could tune in to a BBC station (probably from Cairo area) and capture a bit of world news. I'd listen and type, and listen and type, until I had some "world" news which I could tack to a makeshift bulletin board. The colonel appreciated that and so did the staff. We were literally cut-off from the outside world, so any bit of "news" was welcome indeed.

We were a "unit" only in the sense that we worked together as such. In fact we were a motley assortment, some with uniforms, most without. Some from stateside and some from Europe. But we quickly melded into a bunch of guys, each of which would pitch-in in whatever way necessary to get any task done. I saw a chief master sergeant using a hammer to build a table out of scrap lumber we had saved from wooden crates which had arrived aboard a C-141. I myself had to find ways to "get things done" in the absence of printed Air Force regulations. Let me offer but one example.

One day, after being there about three weeks, it happened that two of our airmen had received messages (via our satellite connection to Ramstein) that they needed to go home on emergency leave. One family death, and one father's emergency heart surgery were the issues. Now, on a normal base, there are established procedures to do such things. But we weren't on a normal base. Far from it. There was but one way we received communications, and that was from a direct satellite feed to our field comm center. This was operated by an Army crew, a major and a captain with whom I had been working quite closely since my arrival. And the only way out of this remote operating base was the same way we came it - a C-141. The two young airmen were from different stateside bases. And to make matters a bit more difficult, their travel-deployment orders had already expired. Since none of us at the outset knew where we would be going, or how long we'd be staying, the various travel orders were vague. Some were valid for 14 days, others for a month. So here stood two young airmen in distress. I knew what had to be done and so I decided to massage the rules a bit so that I could do what I knew the Air Force "would" do in such a case. So I asked the Army major in the comm center tent whether it might be possible to send a message up to the satellite and have it return directly to our location. He said it could be done. So I took the two airmen's expired orders and hammered out on the comm center "typewriter" a message (two actually) amending the travel orders for the two airmen. In the "real" Air Force only the unit preparing the original orders can amend them. I knew that, but I also knew we could not communicate with the original units because officially we - our little American unit in Egypt -- did not exist, and we could not disclose either our "unit" or its location. I also knew that travel orders had three to four rows of coded numbers near the bottom of the page and that those numbers were called "fund cites." In short, those numbers identify which financial accounts are being used to pay for the travel. So I simply copied those numbers onto my "amended" orders and bounced the whole thing off the satellite and back to us so I could print them and get them into the hands of the two airmen. With those "amended" orders and my authorization for emergency leave both airmen could go out of our location aboard one of the outbound C-141s. They'd eventually land at Ramstein or

Rhein Main and from there would be allowed to board flights back to the U.S. Technically, what I did was less than legal at best. But I knew I had done what the Air Force would have done if it had had the opportunity. I never heard back from the two airmen, so I can only guess that they arrived safely. I did tell them as they were leaving that when they returned to their home bases, some admin weenie would be scratching his head trying to figure out how those orders got amended. I told them they could blame some incompetent captain somewhere at an undisclosed location. Eventually it would work out. When the whole thing was done, I briefed my "colonel." He smiled, then laughed in that "we got them" sort of look. He was almost as pleased as I was. I figured all those years as an enlisted guy just paid off. For me it was a challenge, and it was fun. Turns out it was about the only thing about that deployment that was "fun." But there was one other event on that deployment that was far more memorable. And that was the visit by the President of Egypt.

Anwar Sadat and a small contingent of his staff came to visit the base after we had become reasonably stable if not fully operational. On his way out to the flight line to meet the President of Egypt my colonel, knowing that we were minimally staffed and "bare bones" equipped, told me we'd be playing it "by ear" and not to set up anything formal. He sped off and waited half-an-hour or so for Sadat to arrive. While he was gone (again, no cell phones in those days) I got to thinking about the situation. Sadat was head of state of a country with which the U.S. had a formal and long-standing political and economic relationship. This was his base, in his country, and he was taking political risks allowing us to operate within his borders. (That was a salient if not prescient thought, for Sadat was assassinated in October 1981 by extreme radical Muslim opponents to his regime.) (I was back in the states at that time.) So I decided we'd do what we could with what we had. We rounded up about a dozen of our guys who were in uniform (work uniform to be sure, but at least in uniform.) We set up two parallel and reasonably-spaced rows as a "formation." We got our mess sergeant to put together a bowl of fruit and some drinks. Someone came up with a small but visible American flag. No red carpet was available, but we took brooms and swept the sand into neat pathway. And just then, our colonel with Sadat and his staff arrived. We stood at attention, saluted, and did an admirable job with what little we had. Once inside our concrete aircraft shelter, we gathered around and swapped greetings. I reached out and served Sadat a glass of orange juice. The timing was great, because I observed that he swallowed a pill with the juice. And then he began to address us. He was angry and spoke with that anger over what he saw as gross mistreatment of his friend, the Shah of Iran. Sadat told us that country after country had denied the Shah who was literally looking for a place to die in some dignity. (Shah Pahlavi had been overthrown and exiled from Iran. He was seriously ill with cancer and did, indeed, later die in Egypt.)

Meanwhile, the Shah needed a place to serve out his exile. It had become known that the Shah was ill with cancer. With this in mind, the U.S. reluctantly allowed the Shah to enter the U.S. In protest, a group of Iranians seized more than sixty American hostages at the U.S. Embassy in Tehran on November 4, 1979. Khomeini saw this as a chance to demonstrate the new Iranian defiance of Western influence.

The new Iranian government and the Carter Administration of the U.S. entered a standoff that wouldn't end until after Ronald Reagan's inauguration in late January of 1981. There followed pressure of sanctions and oil embargoes imposed by the U.S. on Iran. This became known as the Iranian Hostage Crisis.

And, of course it was this - the Iranian Hostage Crisis - which had resulted in my deployment to Egypt. As for new leadership in Iran:

Ayatollah Khomeini became the supreme religious leader of the Islamic Republic of Iran in 1979, following many years of resistance to Shah Pahlavi. Following his appointment as Ayatollah, Khomeini worked to remove the Shah from power for his associations with the West. Upon the success of the revolution Ayatollah Khomeini was named religious and political leader of Iran for life.

Sadat also told us how concerned he was about a Russian invasion into Afghanistan which had just begun:

The Soviet invasion of Afghanistan began in late December 1979 with troops from the Soviet Union. The Soviet Union had intervened in support of the Afghan communist government in its conflict with anticommunist Muslim guerrillas during the Afghan War (1978–92) and remained in Afghanistan until mid-February 1989.

I offer you these little website clips just to give you a better idea of what the world looked like in late 1979 and how it all came to impact me personally. Much was at stake and listening personally to Sadat at this remote little air base out in a remote desert of Egypt certainly was a memorable experience.

While Sadat was speaking to us I kept surveying the small group of Egyptian officialdom with him.

One stocky, dark-eyed fellow with a cane caught my eye (I thought the cane was fake). I did not know until the day of Sadat's assassination who that other fellow was. Turns out he was Ḥosnī Mubārak, at the time vice president, who later replaced Sadat as President. After an hour or so with us, Sadat and his staff departed as they had come.

When my colonel returned from the flight line, he gave me a wink and said thanks. He knew it was right for us to honor President Sadat with what little we had.

A few days later, the preparations we had been working on became an operational reality when the AWACS landed. Also known as the E-3 Sentry and easy to spot because of its distinctive rotating radar dome above the fuselage, its arrival was our contribution to Operation Eagle Claw.

One day in mid or late January 1980 I returned to Ramstein, gave a briefing to that still secret ops team in the headquarters, then found Josie working in her office. It was a joyful reunion. But that joy was offset by the grief, the embarrassment, the pain, and the agony when Operation Eagle Claw came to a disastrous end April 24, 1980. The 52 hostages were eventually returned when President Ronald Reagan replaced Jimmy Carter.

Still, I was home. Back at Ramstein. And once again up to my ears in projects and events. Among those events were the many receptions and social gatherings with political leaders. Throughout the Ramstein years I found myself invited – as a representative of the U. S. Air Forces in Europe – to join German state governors (they were called Ministerpräsident) and other such dignitaries around Germany. (See invitations.) At more than a few of these events (music, speeches, press coverage, sumptuous tid-bits to nibble on while being seen in the presence of those who are being seen) I happened to become acquainted with some of Berlin's original Trümmerfrauen. These were the women who literally picked up the rubble of war, the broken bricks, the shattered pieces of what had once been buildings. These Trümmerfrauen filled wheelbarrow after wheelbarrow by the millions to clear away war rubble and make way for rebuilding. Even today the results of their work can be seen. There are large hills in and around Germany's major cities where no geological force created them. These hills of rubble have been covered with soil. They became known as Schuttberg, or Trümmerberg. Now they are parks. Thanks to the women, the Trümmerfrauen. As I learned from those women I met – they were members of the Federation of German-American friendship clubs – it was the women of all social backgrounds who did the grunt work to rebuild after the war. I understood the logic. The war had killed and maimed men by the millions. Hence women were left to rebuild. So even though I, as the USAFE representative to that Federation, did not always feel I fit among the social elite, I did appreciate the opportunity to meet many of Germany's historical and political figures.

Looking back, now, even to my early Air Force days at Hahn AB when I was but an enlisted airman, there was one other such occasion I should share. After all, this book about my Air Force career is itself history, right? And my history happens to blend from time to time with world history. Can't be avoided. So, before putting to rest this section on Germany, let me briefly take you back to Hahn Air Base around 1962, even before Josie and I had met. Our base had an active Boy Scout troop. Someone came up with the idea of making Germany's Chancellor Konrad Adenauer an "honorary Eagle Scout." For starters you'll need to know just a bit about Konrad Adenauer. He was Germany's first Chancellor (equivalent to President) following World War II. As the first democratically-elected leader in the aftermath of the Hitler era, the eyes of the world as well as those of his nation were upon him. He was popularly known as "Der Alte" (German: the old one). He began his office as Chancellor at the age of 73, and he remained in office 14 years, until 1963. And thanks to those Boy Scouts at Hahn Air Base, I had the opportunity to personally meet Der Alte. I travelled to Bonn, then the seat of government, with the scouts and a small contingent from our base. As our base commander and the scouts presented the Eagle Scout sash to Der Alte, the German press crowded around to capture the moment with photos (the old flash- bulb type cameras). Unfortunately, our photographer - a female staff sergeant who normally shot only portraits for passports - did not get "her shot" of the event and began to cry. She didn't just weep. She wailed in tears. And this caught the attention of Der Alte, not to mention the attention of our base commander, who was "mortified" to put it mildly. Der Alte asked what was the matter, what had happened? Our sergeant explained, still in tears, that "those guys," referring to the crush of media, were pushing and shoving and she could not get a picture. So Der Alte stood and addressed the news photographers and told them in stern German to back away. They did. And the whole event was re-staged while our photographer got her picture. Pop! Flash! And the media guys got their pictures ... of her getting her picture ... Pop! Flash! Der Alte spoke a bit, shook hands with all of us, and all was well. Sort of. Until the next day when we saw the German newspapers! The picture of our sergeant getting her picture and the caption explaining the set-up and the tears! And right there I – a budding journalist – learned the difference between "good press" and "bad press." And I knew that our photographer was in deep hot water with our commander. Her career as photo-journalist ended that day.

As far as I know, she never again took any photos other than portraits for passports. As for Der Alte, he was a gentleman as well as a great politician who led Germany out of the ashes of war and into an economic powerhouse known as "Wirtschaftswunder," German for "economic miracle." And I had had the opportunity to meet Konrad Adenauer while learning two of the rules of journalism: never cry while doing photo-journalism, and never embarrass your base commander! What a memory!

So as my assignment to Ramstein Air Base came to an end, I found myself reflecting. I had had a great deal of hands-on involvement with the Cold War. I had also experienced the beginnings of the next era of warfare as the Iran Hostage event exploded into a new form of conflict, that of terrorism and extremism. So when we took-off from Rhein Main AB aboard our flight back to the United States, I took a deep breath and let out a sigh of relief. Ramstein had been, indeed, a gut-wrenching experience. Next stop. Indiana. Fort Benjamin Harrison.

Assigned to an Army Base, 1981, Then Retirement

My final Air Force assignment was 1981-1985 on an Army base. Yes, the Cold War was still underway, but the pace at this new base was much slower, less intense. Why? Well, for starters this was an academic environment. My assignment was to the Defense Information School located on Fort Benjamin Harrison, on the far east side of Indianapolis. I had acquired substantial experience in the public affairs career field, and at "Fort Ben" I was to use this experience as an instructor. The school - known locally as Dinfos - was the Department of Defense training institute for radio-television broadcasters, journalists, and public affairs officers. The students and teaching staff were officers and enlisted men of all services: Army, Navy, Marines, Air Force, and Coast Guard. I had attended this school as an Air Force lieutenant immediately following my 1970 commissioning in San Antonio. Now, eleven years later, I was back as an instructor. Technically I was an assistant professor.

The school was accredited as a college, meaning that our students gained college credits which could be transferred to any college or university in the country. So, technically I was an assistant college professor. My students were both officers and enlisted men. Each officer class also had a number of foreign allied students. I had students from

Saudi Arabia and from Egypt, from the Philippines and Japan, from Germany and Luxembourg, and from other countries. I taught courses in public affairs and community relations.

I taught about NATO and Western Europe - from which I had just returned following my Ramstein assignment. I taught concepts in community relations, and also community relations and the environment. At the outset, even though I was well-grounded in these academic areas, I often found myself feeling somewhat intimidated because many of my students were officers who literally outranked me. I was a major, but in each class I had students who were Lt Colonels and even "full" Colonels. Often I also had students who were Ph. D.'s not to mention many with masters' degrees. After a while, I came to recognize that although these "students" had degrees well beyond my own, they did not have the experience equivalent to mine, nor did they have degrees within my field. Once I got by that stumbling block, I did quite well as an instructor.

I suppose what I was doing was not unlike what any teacher would be doing in any classroom environment, except for one minor detail. In each "classroom hour" of instruction, I had to have a folder at a designated desk in the rear of the classroom. Within that folder was my "neatly typewritten" and very detailed lesson plan. I would be visited by evaluators - the Commandant, the Deputy Commandant, or the Department Chief. Woe to the instructor who had wandered off topic when the Commandant took his seat at the evaluator desk! Woe to the instructor whose lesson plan was deemed inadequate! Woe to the instructor if the Commandant could not readily find the topic under discussion within that plan! So, there was a fair amount of stress in that teaching environment. But it was nothing like the stress in the day-to-day work environment with NATO forces in Europe where the consequences of failure could be catastrophic! That was stress. But, to my great relief, I never received a negative comment from my evaluators while I was teaching at Dinfos.

About midway through the four-year assignment at Fort Ben, I had to have surgery on my spine. That pretty well signaled that the end of my career was just around the bend. I had been flown via medical airlift to the Air Force hospital at San Antonio for the surgery. Seventeen days in the hospital. Then 45 days recovery at home. I did return to duty and continued teaching. But there would be no further assignments. It was time to put a wrap on my Air Force career.

A major Bonus to an Air Force Career

I entered the Air Force in June 1961 with a high school diploma. I left the Air Force in 1985 with one Bachelor's Degree (English) from U. of Nebraska at Omaha, a second Bachelor's Degree (German) from U. of Maryland, and a Master of Science Degree (Radio-TV) from Butler University. At Butler, I also minored in education and used that to obtain my teaching certification, Indiana. All of that helped me step out of the Air Force and into teaching German and English for my second career. But that's another book. Maybe.

About the Author

Author Frank Tilton is an amalgam of curiosity, careers, and continual education. Now a retired middle school teacher of German and English, Tilton was first a career U.S. Air Force officer. The California native enlisted in the Air Force at age 17. Nine years later he became a commissioned officer. He served NATO in Europe and Air Defense forces in the United States. Throughout his 24-year USAF career, he continued "cracking the books." By the time he was ready to launch his second career, teaching, he had garnered one bachelor's degree in German, another in English/Journalism, and a master's degree in Radio/Television. At age 42 Tilton shed the Air Force blue uniform and spent the next 19 years in middle school classrooms educating well over 2,000 teenagers. Now retired from teaching, Tilton has authored six books. His recent release, *Eternity: a scholarly yet lighthearted look at life's biggest question* is now available from Amazon.com as are his other books. He is married to the former Josefine Lohse of Germany and has two grown children and four grandchildren.

-30-

Made in the USA
Middletown, DE
03 March 2020